Lost and Turned Out

A Guide to Preparing Underserved Communities for Disaster

VINCENT B. DAVIS

LOST AND TURNED OUT

DEDICATION

This book is dedicated to my dear mother
Elizabeth and my late father George Allen Davis.

CONTENTS

ACKNOWLEDGMENTS

Praise to my personal Lord and Savior Jesus The Christ, through whom all things are possible.

Thanks to my children, Deila, Brian, Raven, Eraina and Felicia, each of whom has inspired and encouraged me in this endeavor.

To my dear friend and mentor Dr. Leon Dingle, Jr.
I am forever grateful for your wisdom, counsel, and guidance.

To my new friend and colleague Jason Ferguson, your energy and passion are gifts from God.

For my wife Maria, the love of my life. Your support has been the inspiration behind my every success. Thank you for sharing this journey.

FOREWORD

Lost and Turned Out provides vital insight into the subtle nuances of the U.S. disaster relief system. Furthermore, it outlines practical approaches to begin to shape a culture of preparedness in underserved communities. This book, however, is not an analysis of the issues affecting minorities or the poor, or a commentary about the sad saga of Hurricane Katrina. Lost and Turned Out is an effort to set the record straight about why the underserved suffer disproportionately during disasters. More important, it offers realistic ideas for what the underserved must do if they are to survive in the future. Today's disaster challenges provide a unique opportunity to re-define clear roles and responsibilities of all stakeholders, and rectify mistakes of the past. Meeting these challenges will require the collective efforts of stakeholders from key institutions; the faith-based community, emergency managers, politicians, community leaders, and yes, the underserved themselves, if we expect to resolve the preparedness dilemma. The burdens created by dwindling disaster funds and the increasing frequency of disasters, make it a matter of utmost urgency for communities to "get real" about disaster preparedness. This book gives candid answers about the reasons underserved communities are unprepared, and examines proven initiatives that we can learn from to help bridge the preparedness gap. Rather than creating a wish list of what others should do, Lost and Turned Out focuses on what the underserved must do to help themselves survive.

CHAPTER 1

THE CASE FOR PREPAREDNESS

"Not everything that is faced can be changed, but nothing can be changed until it is faced."

James Baldwin

The bloated corpse of an elderly woman lay motionless on the hard concrete. Eyes open, her face was partially covered with a filthy rag. As I stared frozen in disbelief at the image on my TV, people casually walked past the woman, barely noticing the lifeless body that lay in their path. My first impression of this scene is it was a report of events from a third-world country. I imagined this news originated from Haiti, the underdeveloped nations of Africa, or perhaps some other island nation in the Caribbean. My shock and dismay turned to downright disgust when the television announcer revealed the location of this picture of death and devastation; New Orleans, Louisiana…USA.

Hurricane Katrina in the 2005 Atlantic hurricane season was the costliest natural disaster, and one of the five deadliest hurricanes in history. Among recorded Atlantic hurricanes, it was the sixth strongest overall. At least 1,836 people died in the actual hurricane and in the flood that followed, making Katrina the deadliest U.S. hurricane since 1928. Katrina exposed a myth many Americans, and much of the world had come to believe; that the U.S. was exempt from the devastating consequences of natural

7

disasters because of superior preparedness. The images of people climbing on rooftops and suffering in the sweltering heat at the Superdome and Convention Center exposed America's true vulnerability to disasters. More important, Katrina uncovered not only how broken the U.S. disaster preparedness system is, but how unprepared the average American, particularly the African-American underclass is to cope with disasters.

The socioeconomic impact of disasters on the poor, elderly, children and other vulnerable populations has long been the subject of discussion amongst politicians, social agencies, and others. When disaster strikes, the underserved are disproportionately affected, and today this remains a blemish on America's image as a country that takes care of its own. Conventional wisdom would lead us to believe underserved populations suffer chiefly as a result of insufficient assets. If this were true, lack of preparedness among the underserved could easily be attributed societal shortcomings in solving the poverty problem. Lack of finances is certainly one influence that contributes to the inadequacy of preparedness, however, other factors must also be considered. Economics alone cannot explain the real issue; the entire nation appears to be indifferent about disasters, and we lag far behind other developed countries in citizen preparedness, especially for the underserved.

In recent debates about the widening gap between Wall Street and Main Street, the conversation has focused mainly on the plight of the shrinking middle-class, and the accumulation of wealth enjoyed by the "one percent". Suffice to say, at the crossroads of those two opposing viewpoints is another thoroughfare known as "Railroad Street". According to Lieutenant General Russell L. Honoré, the retired U.S. Army leader who took charge of the Katrina rescue effort, Railroad St. is any place where the underprivileged reside. It was in this imaginary place that America's weak disaster preparedness posture was fully displayed, during the spectacle that unfolded after Hurricane Katrina.

It is noteworthy that African-Americans made up the vast majority of Hurricane Katrina's victims. Many of them were economically disadvantaged, uneducated, underemployed and living in relative obscurity until the storm. Despite the nation's vast resources, forgotten pockets of poverty, such as those found in Louisiana, still exist. Nevertheless many Americans seemed shocked when they witnessed thousands of poor people stranded, fighting for their lives. General Honoré directed the rescue effort in New Orleans days after floods ravaged the city. He immediately described earlier rescue efforts as the activities of people stuck on stupid. One of General Honoré's initial actions was to order National Guard troops and law enforcement officers to lower their weapons, reminding them Katrina was indeed a rescue mission not a combat zone.

If America expects to reverse the plight of the underserved during disasters, we need to begin an honest dialogue about the factors that influence the lopsided impact catastrophes continue to have on the "Railroad Street" inhabitants of our society.

Although the reasons for lack of preparedness are complex, the solutions are straightforward. First and foremost the true reasons underserved populations are not prepared must be thoroughly examined by all members of the community. This includes not only first responders and emergency managers, but community organizations, faith-based groups, businesses, and nongovernmental disaster relief partners, must be part of the discussion. Secondly, we must implement new approaches to educate, inform, and prepare underserved communities to effectively cope with the realities of disasters.

Accomplishing these two fundamental goals is essential if we hope to break the cycle of government dependence that renders the underserved powerless in the face of catastrophes. The alternative is a repeat of Katrina, which is inevitable if we continue on the present course.

In some ways, the underserved may be their own nemesis when it comes to preparing for disasters. The preparedness gap between poor blacks, Latinos, and whites is significant. This gap has a profound impact on each group's survival rate in a disaster. Dr. Damon T. Arnold, Director of the Masters of Public Health Program at Chicago State University, and former Director of the Illinois Department of Public Health, defines a disaster as any circumstance which seriously compromises one's ability to cope.

How we cope with the aftermath of disasters has little to do with how well government responders and relief organizations carry out their roles. By creating well prepared communities, we can assure underserved people can take care of themselves and others *before* a catastrophe strikes. My purpose for writing this book is to debunk some misconceptions about the disaster system, and to educate and inform readers about preparedness. The title Lost and Turned Out originated from the R&B group The Whispers popular 1970's song 'Olivia'. The song is about a naive young woman who gets taken advantage of by a slick and ruthless street hustler. Indeed, as the song relates in its hook, Olivia lost her way and was turned out. Disadvantaged populations are similarly victimized by a disaster system they do not thoroughly understand, and this is the moral anecdote to be derived from the song. Paralyzed by their own fear and lack of information about what preparedness entails, the underserved are even more vulnerable during disasters. Today, seven years after Hurricane Katrina, and more than a decade removed from the horror of September 11, 2001 the underserved are still not prepared.

They stroll naively into the next disaster, continuing to believe the government will take care of them. By doing so, they are gambling with their survival. Middle income Americans by and large possess sufficient resources to cope with the aftermath of most disasters. Although the middle class, or for that matter the wealthy, do not necessarily recognize the need to prepare, the consequences of this indifference are much more severe for people below the poverty level.

A case in point; if one has a credit card and a motor vehicle, evacuation is merely an inconvenience. For the underserved, disaster situations can be life changing events. It is ironic the poor and underserved have the most to lose yet are the least prepared. Human survival, not property losses, should be the primary goal of everyone in disasters. Despite limited finances, underserved populations are not using many of the options available to adequately prepare themselves.

In a speech at a Chicago disaster event in 2009, General Honoré added clarity to the preparedness topic. He pointed out the link between one's ability to survive a disaster with preparedness actions taken *before* the disaster. During Hurricane Katrina, and more recent disasters like Hurricane Irene in 2011, and Hurricane Isaac in 2012, the lack of preparedness of the underserved was painfully apparent. Preparedness is the key to surviving catastrophes. Those who survive catastrophes as horrific as the World Trade Center terrorist attack, or a single house fire, more often than not share a common attribute that increases their chances for survival.....**Preparedness**.

Despite what many believe, the U.S. disaster system is alive and well. Unfortunately, most Americans reinforced their inaccurate beliefs about the disaster system based on what they saw on TV during Hurricane Katrina. What occurred behind the headlines and sound bites may come as a shock to many.

Through countless experiences in the National Guard, at FEMA and the American Red Cross, this author witnessed first-hand the incredible devastation of 11 major disasters. Through these experiences, many valuable lessons were learned about disasters and preparedness. While I shall not attempt to justify the failures of government or others, I will offer some perspective about the events of the past eleven years, and put forward solutions to help the underserved survive in the future.

CHAPTER 2

HOW THE UNDERSERVED GOT PLAYED –A HISTORICAL PERSPECTIVE

"If a sufficient number of management layers are superimposed on top of each other, it can be assured that disaster is not left to chance."

Norman Ralph Augustine

Historically, the ten most costly catastrophes in U.S. history were all natural disasters--seven of them hurricanes. All occurred since 1989, a period which Congress referred to as The Decade for Natural Disaster Reduction. Why was this tremendous period so destructive to communities? Although some blame Mother Nature, environmental historian Ted Steinberg explained much of the death and destruction has been well within the realm of human control. In his book Acts of God, Steinberg exposes the mistake of seeing such catastrophes as mere random events. Steinberg explores the history of natural disasters, and the decisions of business leaders and government officials contributing to greater losses of life and property, especially among America's poor, elderly, and minorities. To blame nature or God as the primary culprit, Steinberg argues, has helped to disguise the fact that, in truth, some Americans are better protected from the violence of nature than their counterparts lower down the socioeconomic ladder. Steinberg questions why the hardest hit areas are frequently mobile home parks and low-income neighborhoods.

In the Cold War era, the civil defense system held responsibility for disaster response. The federal government spent considerable amounts of time and effort to prepare citizens for a nuclear holocaust at the hands of America's Eastern European foe, the Soviet Union. They erected elaborate bomb shelters in public buildings and provided public service messages about where to go if the powerful bomb hit. In its infancy, racism in the civil defense system resulted in low participation in drills and evacuation exercises by African-Americans. These societal ills were more prevalent in the Deep South where African-Americans were denied the opportunity to serve as auxiliary police officers, firefighters, or to participate in civil defense training. The types of preparedness behaviors and attitudes in which African-Americans have today can be somewhat explained by these early obstacles.

As a child, I vividly recall the bomb shelter drills at school. Herding us into the basement bomb shelter was the main step taken to prepare us for nuclear attack. When I was in fourth grade, a gas explosion at a home near the school so traumatized us that some children, (myself included) wet their pants, terrified we were about to die in a nuclear holocaust.

The Cold War era ushered in a period of dependence during which the government sent a clear message to all Americans; we'll take care of everyone if something terrible happens. This trend toward government responsibility started under the Eisenhower administration with the building of the interstate highway system and continued through the next several decades. Coincidentally, the government built the interstate system to provide an interconnected pathway for movement of military convoys across the country. Convenience of travel to grandmas during the holidays did not figure in their decision.

The creation of FEMA in 1979 resulted from failed local government responses to Hurricane Floyd. Civil Defense Councils, which were previously a state controlled enterprise, had proved to be ineffective. Government's nurtured citizen dependency because they believed that ordinary citizens had no idea how to take care of themselves in a catastrophe. Underserved communities became the chief recipients of this philosophy, an excess which was a sign of the times. Millions of dollars were funneled into poor, predominantly black communities during the early 1960's a period dubbed as President Lyndon B. Johnson's 'War on Poverty'. Presumably these funds were to create jobs and close the poverty gap resulting from years of Jim Crow segregation.

Government intervention became the preferred method to cure the systematic racism which had left many African-Americans uneducated and underemployed. An unwanted side effect of this strategy caused the poor to become dependent. Public housing programs bred a welfare mentality, even though these "projects" gave black ghettoes an upgrade from existing substandard housing.

Born in Chicago's Ida B. Wells public housing project, this

author recognizes the intent of public housing was honorable. Poor oversight of the housing developments would ultimately lead to immediate problems. Issues abounded, including poor maintenance and supervision of the buildings and lax screening of tenants. Lack of affordable housing remained only part of the challenges black families faced in the 1960's. Poverty stricken families were supposed to have a clean, quiet refuge from drugs, crime and gang activity, but this was not to be the case.

Taking care of the whole community involves more than merely putting a roof over people's heads. Joblessness, discrimination, lack of educational opportunity, and public aid rules fractured the foundation of many black families. Black men frequently abandoned their families in order to ensure they would receive food stamps. Welfare rules required husbands and father's be absent from home in order for their children to receive benefits. Alcoholism, drug abuse, and domestic violence echoed the frustration and futility many black men felt. The dejection and hopelessness experienced by grown men who failed to keep their families together would haunt a generation of African-Americans.

By the early 1970's, blacks took advantage of newly opened job opportunities resulting from Affirmative Action laws. These changes opened occupations in companies where minorities were previously barred, or had only a token representation. It is a mistake to believe these programs were a handout. The only thing most people of humble beginnings want is an opportunity. This author was the recipient of such opportunities, becoming the first African-American cable splicer technician in one of Chicago's largest suburban districts for Illinois Bell Telephone Company. Doors which were previously closed suddenly opened, providing a path for us and future generations to pursue meaningful careers. My children have been recipients of these open doors, earning multiple degrees from prestigious institutions such as Brown, Yale, Notre Dame, Michigan and Boston College. Each is engaged in positive pursuits, and their success comes from hard work, focus, and *opportunity*. For many blacks of my generation, however, chances would come too little too late. Many succumbed to the mean streets, or were derailed from their dreams to lead unfulfilled lives. My family happened to be one of the fortunate few who escaped the projects in the early 1960's. We were able to leave the inner city by the grace of God. My dad worked two full-time jobs, and my determined mother did housework for many of the white families whose descendants are my neighbors today.

For my two older brothers and me, growing up in the suburbs had its own set of challenges, but it gave us access to a quality education, of which we took full advantage. It also offered us a haven from constant exposure to crime, drugs, and despair that were commonplace in many inner-city neighborhoods.

History would later reveal the mistake of stacking poor people on top of each other in concrete buildings with little structure or chance for upward mobility. Lessons learned from the drug and gang infestation of the projects, and lack of upward mobility, foreshadowed the end of housing projects in the late 1990's. These changes were part of a neighborhood revitalization that began in the late 1980s and continued throughout the next two decades. By the time the wrecking balls demolished Cabrini Green, the last of Chicago's notorious public housing projects, a quiet shift was also taking place in how the government viewed disaster relief.

The moral of this story is that underserved communities, the same as "project kids", should never be written off as lazy or unmotivated to want to improve their condition. Most underserved populations would embrace a culture of preparedness, but do not know how to go about creating it. They can succeed in changing their situation and become prepared, only if given a genuine opportunity to attain the skills and knowledge required to make happen. The late Godfather of Soul, James Brown, stated it best in his popular tune written during the pinnacle of the Civil Rights movement; *"I Don't Want Nobody To Give Me Nothin', Open Up Door, And I'll Get It Myself."*

What one does not know will hurt them. In 2002 as a direct consequence of the September 11th terror attacks, the Department of Homeland Security (DHS) came into existence. It combined 22 existing federal agencies, including the U.S. Coast Guard, Customs and Border Patrol, FEMA, and others under one umbrella. The formation of DHS also brought about creation of the Transportation Security Administration, (TSA) to oversee airport security. To fund DHS Congress appropriated billions of dollars, a large portion allocated from existing agency budgets. Some of these funds were spent organizing the new department. First responders received substantial grants to obtain needed equipment and training. Citizen preparedness initiatives also benefitted from DHS funding. The formation of DHS ushered in a new era in which the government began distancing itself from its previous strategy of citizen dependency. After years of increasing expenditures on disaster relief, and greater scrutiny by Congress of federal disaster funds, the game changed.

Unlike in the past, the Government was not pretending to be the savior. The new, more realistic message was; we'll help when we can, but be prepared to go it alone for at least 72 hours before federal resources can be brought to bear. In the past decade because of budget cuts, cash strapped state and local governments are increasingly incapable of paying for recovery costs from calamities. By 2005, the message that the government is not the answer to your immediate survival had become increasingly clear in nearly every community experiencing frequent disasters. Most people got it, but poor, underserved communities missed the memo and remained stuck in the government dependent mode of the 1950's and 60's.

Even today, most states have no funds set aside to help people recover from disasters. Too often, states engage in a hopeful mentality when it comes to disaster programs. When a disaster happens they hope it is severe enough to qualify for a FEMA declaration. Meanwhile, several recent reports indicate the number of Americans living in poverty has been on the rise. This trend does not bode well for helping underserved communities prepare for disasters.

Many households have seen incomes decline as their expenses and debts continue to increase. In the past few years, more than 15% of the population lived in poverty, the highest percentage since 1993, according to the most recent data from the U.S. Census Bureau. To put it into perspective, this means more than 46 million people fell below the poverty line, defined as $22,314 per year for a family of four. If one considers in the income spent on expenses like medical costs, child care and mortgage payments, the number of Americans whose remaining income falls below the poverty line is closer to 50 million, or roughly 16% of the population.

As severe as this seems, some regions in the U.S. are much worse off. In the 2010 Census a breakdown of the poverty rate in every county in the U.S., showed dozens of counties where more than a third of the population lives in poverty and a handful whose overall poverty rates were closer to 50%. The data focused on 15 counties with the highest overall poverty rates in the country. About half of the counties on the list are in the South, where the jobless rate is higher than the national average, at more than 9%.

How does poverty factor into the disaster relief system? The United States Department of Commerce (USDC, 2000) reports

African-Americans with incomes less than $15,000 per year are unlikely to have Internet access at home. Thus, lack of Internet access and usage may limit levels of preparedness for disasters among low-income African-Americans. Other variables, such as access to CPR training, could also be identified as potential problems in the examination of preparedness behavior.

The year before Katrina, this author managed a FEMA Community Relations team in Michigan responding to floods affecting thousands of basements in Detroit and surrounding communities. Wayne County, which includes Detroit and surrounding suburbs, was the most affected because of its dense population. The response strategy was formed at a meeting with the FEMA Federal Coordinating Officer (FCO) and officials from the State of Michigan and City of Detroit. The goal was to head off anticipated unrest due to changes in the disaster relief process for individuals and households. The issue was that since the last substantial Detroit flood occurred in 2002, FEMA's belt had tightened. New rules were in place which permitted FEMA only to pay for essential damage. FEMA defined this as damage to furnaces, water heaters, washers, dryers, and foundation structural repairs. FEMA no longer regarded basements as living space thus it would not pay claims for things like pool tables, personal clothing, electronics, furniture, or other items commonly found in many Midwest basements. During previous disasters, FEMA paid for claims for personal property items damaged in basements. Reportedly FEMA paid almost any damage claim in the 2002 flood. Rules were so lax that one local official told me the prevailing slogan in the neighborhoods was dial 800 to get $800, meaning FEMA paid smaller claims without question.

Detroit residents would be in for a rude awakening because they were unaware of the new rules. By 2005, in a part of the country where residents routinely use their basements for additional living space, the change meant they would no longer be compensated for personal property losses in rooms below the first floor. My mission in Detroit was to coordinate with local public officials, community leaders, and state officials to try and head off anticipated unrest when FEMA revealed news about the rule changes. The anticipated negative reaction, which officials feared may turn violent, prompted orders for extra security at disaster recovery centers in the city. Assaults against FEMA inspectors by upset residents were a well-founded concern. Reducing friction between the government and the residents of Detroit became the primary objective of the operation.

The quantity of unqualified applications among the 80,000 anticipated needed to be reduced, thus allowing those who had valid damage claims to be processed more quickly. Unwittingly, my daughter Deila, (who prior to the disaster had worked as a Policy Analyst for the Detroit City Council), became a key asset in the public relations strategy. Through her relationships, this author had become acquainted with several prominent city leaders prior to joining FEMA. Despite their misgivings about FEMA, and open animosity toward state officials, Detroit city leaders trusted my daughter, and because of this were willing to work with me. As a result, bitterly opposing factions of government agreed to put aside their differences to help push out the message to the affected communities. To prevent thousands of Detroit residents from standing in long lines at disaster recovery centers only to be denied assistance under the new rules, we worked hard to craft special public service announcements. We also conducted dozens of community meetings to set expectations. Success in this instance meant no FEMA staff became targets of violence during the recovery. For me, however, the outcome was bittersweet. When our team departed Detroit we were all aware that people were still unprepared for the next disaster.

The fact that the African-American population of Detroit remained clueless as to the FEMA rule changes, and lacked understanding on how to navigate the federal and state disaster relief systems, profoundly disturbed me. At the outset of the recovery effort in Detroit, it became apparent an absence of preparedness existed, causing people to wake up to water filled basements. Homeowners could have taken steps to mitigate the damage if they were more informed before the flood. This was even more troubling given the fact Detroit had already experienced considerable flooding just a few years earlier. In the Motor City, as in many other poor communities, apathy, indifference, and reliance on government were prevalent. Following the federal declaration, the State funded some limited programs to offset FEMA gaps.

Unfortunately, most Detroit residents either did not bother to apply or failed to qualify for the programs.

Like many average citizens, this writer had never experienced a disaster first hand. Part of my role as FEMA's External Affairs manager involved supervising Community Relations teams. These teams consist of people who go to homes and businesses in the affected areas to provide information regarding FEMA and state disaster programs. As a member of the Regional Administrator's staff, managing community outreach programs in Illinois, Indiana, Ohio, Michigan, Wisconsin, and Minnesota was a key part of my responsibilities. To perform these tasks, I not only needed to understand the agency's policies, but I also had to be well versed on the entire range of activities associated with local, state and federal disaster programs.

Actually, prior to Detroit, my first deployment with FEMA was to southeastern Ohio near the West Virginia border. The President had approved Federal disaster assistance after ice storms ravaged the southern portion of the state. Arriving on the first day after the declaration, I met with the county emergency manager in a makeshift office located in a converted storefront. Unaware of the nuances of the business of disasters, I had no idea what to expect. The county was poor, predominantly white, and a large percentage of residents lived below national poverty levels. The county emergency manager, a down-to-earth, single mother of three children, greeted me warmly in her tiny office. Aside from her role managing disaster relief, she had a full-time job of managing public safety programs, which she intimated paid little but provided steady work.

Together we outlined a plan to deploy joint FEMA/County teams into the community. The process involved going door-to-door to inform people about FEMA programs approved under the federal declaration. Many of the houses in the county consisted of trailers and "shotgun" one-room shacks. The emergency manager affectionately spoke of her county as 'Little Appalachia' in reference to its poor, white population. Indeed, as I would discover over the next few weeks, the county's residents were proud, independent people who lived ordinary lives. Some county residents had never even seen an African-American in person until this author showed up at their doorstep to discuss FEMA relief programs.

The county emergency manager's knowledge of her role, and those of the State and FEMA, tremendously impressed me. Her familiarity with the programs, processes, paperwork, and pitfalls of the system was apparent as she quickly set about the task of coordinating relief efforts. Her expertise allowed her to be skillful in assisting her neighbors with the bureaucratic process of obtaining disaster relief. The contrasts between this disaster, and my Detroit experience were striking. 'Little Appalachia" survivors took an active role in the application process, and were well informed about their role in the process. The significance of these facts is something I failed to grasp until much later. Although their experience with recovery from the ice storms was unpleasant, it lacked noticeable bitterness found in the Detroit floods. In the latter, many residents left disappointed and angry, believing the system had failed them once again. To be sure, the people of "Little Appalachia" started at the low end of the economic spectrum before the disaster and were still there afterward. What made their recovery less painful turned out to be the fact they had an advocate who understood the system, and they made it a personal priority to engage in the disaster process.

Another fact everyone needs to understand is contrary to popular belief; FEMA's role in administering assistance is not to make people whole. If one becomes a disaster survivor, it is not reasonable to expect any relief program to help recover all your losses. The goal of disaster relief is to provide a path to recovery, but recovery does not mean reinstatement. No matter what, life will never be the same as before the disaster, and one is likely to suffer some unrecoverable losses.

What also impressed me were the small mitigation actions many Ohio residents undertook before the disaster. Some residents had obtained dry ice from local merchants, which helped prevent food spoilage during expected power outages. Others placed paving stones to create walkways over icy front yard ponds. Many residents had even placed makeshift sandbags around their homes. The purpose of the sandbags was to guard against flooding they knew would occur when the temperatures increased.

After the Ohio disaster, I truly understood preparedness is a choice; not dependent on how many resources one has, but on how people use what they have in the most practical way possible. How could a poor community in southern Ohio be resilient and knowledgeable about disasters, while a likewise impoverished community in Detroit was so unprepared?

The answer can be summed up in three key areas that are the foundations of personal preparedness:

(1) Awareness of potential hazards

(2) Understanding of the disaster system, and

(3) Willingness to make a personal commitment to preparedness.

The coming together of these factors made the difference between a disaster of inconvenience in Ohio, and one of enormous despair and catastrophic loss in Detroit. The book Acts of God, which I referred to earlier, chronicles the failures of the U.S. disaster system, and exposes its relationship to how funding and programs are designed to keep poor communities from breaking out of the cycle of repeated losses. Acts of God is a must read for anyone who cares to understand the socioeconomic aspects of the U.S. disaster system. It provides keen insight as to why poor communities such as "Little Appalachia" in Ohio are destined to deal with the ills of the system which rewards the well-to-do.

The same (Federal) system intended to help people continues

year after year to ignore the causes contributing to neighborhoods who suffer repetitive losses. For this reason, what happened in Hurricane Katrina should not have been a shock to poor Americans. Because they depended on an inadequate levee system, it only proves how disconnected citizens of New Orleans were about the risks they faced before the event.

Preparedness actions the underserved population of New Orleans could have taken leading up to Katrina did not occur to them. This somewhat explains why the outcome in New Orleans doomed the underserved to defeat well before the storm.

Summary Characteristics of the Underserved

Individuals living below Poverty

- Focused on immediate day-to- day needs and preparedness is not a priority.
- Financially unable to make or maintain a disaster kit.
- Disaster planning is not a priority.
- May not have alternate shelter or family situation to evacuate.
- May have limited or no access to transportation

Homeless

- No permanent address to receive benefits or information
- Focused on immediate day-to-day survival
- Increased likelihood of mental illness or substance abuse

issues

- Unaccompanied minors may be in this group
- Limited English Proficiency (LEP)
- During evacuation and while in shelters, may not understand instructions if not provided in their primary language
- May not understand instructions for building a kit or making a plan if not provided in their primary language

Undocumented

- May be unwilling to follow government or disaster relief organizations instructions or fully participate in registration
- Reluctant to seek assistance from disaster relief organizations because of fears of deportation

Populations with Cultural Differences

- Cultural differences may require men and women must be separated
- Dietary restrictions may create additional shelter and mass care challenges

Elderly

- Higher percentage of people with functional needs
- May have difficulty understanding and following directions of first responders and care givers
- Increased need for health services (e.g., medications and medical equipment, nursing staff)
- May not have their own personal transportation

Children

- More likely to be separated from family
- Trauma may result in more long term effects due to a limited capacity to cope and understand
- Unaccompanied minors have implications for sheltering and family reunification

People with Functional Needs

- May have mobility issues, hearing or sight impairment possible
- Higher probability for health and medical needs
- May be unable to stay in a group shelter or self-evacuate
- May have chronic physical or mental health needs

People with no motor vehicle

- Unable to self-evacuate
- Require transport to and from shelters

CHAPTER 3

THE TRUTH ABOUT HURRICANE KATRINA

Americans rightly asked," if this is the way our government responds to a natural disaster it knew about days in advance, how would it respond to a surprise terrorist attack? How would it respond to an earthquake?"

Russ Carnahan

New Orleans mayor Ray Nagin reportedly received almost 20 million dollars more than a year before Hurricane Katrina to establish a workable evacuation plan. Whether a plan was ever developed is questionable, and if so, the plan was never distributed. Two months before Katrina, Nagin reportedly spent money to produce and distribute DVDs in poor neighborhoods to inform residents that they would be on their own if a storm hit because the city could not afford to evacuate them.

The following factors also contributed to the tragedy:

* 55% did not possess a car or a way to evacuate

* 68% had no money in the bank, or useable credit card

* 57% had total household incomes of less than $20,000 in the prior year

* 76% had children under 18 with them in the shelter

* 77% had a high school education or less

* 93% were African-American

* 67% were employed full or part-time before the hurricane

Nearly 40% of those who died were elderly. No statistics are available for elderly individuals who died later from the stress of evacuation and home loss. The 30,000 people who evacuated to the Superdome (per Nagin's instructions) became stranded for a week. Superdome evacuees experienced deplorable conditions; unbearable heat, darkness, nonfunctioning restroom facilities, and a lack of food, water, and first aid.

The most unforgivable failure in this author's opinion occurred when Governor Blanco failed activate Louisiana National Guard troops. They were badly needed at the Superdome to provide security for the thousands stranded. During Hurricane Katrina, a parade of New Orleans' marginalized left behind citizens was dumped to fend for themselves in the Superdome. Some were elderly people, so frail they were barely able to walk. The crowd also included mothers with infants, stranded vacationers whose hotels had closed, down-and-out citizens, drug addicts, criminals, and homeless people. None had a chance of getting out of town, and no shelters but the Superdome and Convention Center that became horror houses of misery. Rapes, assaults, and horrendous acts were committed by predators inside the dome that were released from flooded city jails.

The real blame for this shameful scene was sorely misplaced. The American public believed media spin that FEMA was somehow in charge. The truth is, however, the responsibility for evacuating, sheltering, mass care, and public safety belonged to the state and local governments. Six people died at the Superdome.

One man is alleged to have thrown himself from an upper seating area. At least one person succumbed to a drug overdose. Four others died of natural causes. Police were credited with stopping an attempted rape, but the lack of significant police presence meant other assaults likely went unreported.

Why then, did the media heap finger pointing at FEMA, President Bush, and FEMA Director Mike Brown? A few basic facts will explain the absurdity of the situation. For starters, most people do not understand FEMA's role and responsibilities in disasters. If the mainstream media had not been so eager to take the easy route, they would have initiated the discussion of what went wrong by explaining the Robert T. Stafford Act. This is the law governing FEMA's rules and authorities, which is covered in greater detail in a later chapter.

Many members of the media understood what occurred, but chose to make a soap opera of the federal response their lead story because it made the drama more sensational.

Throughout the ordeal, not one reporter ever asked Mayor Nagin, (while he screamed at President Bush like a two-year-old having a tantrum) why he did not order an organized evacuation of the hospitals, nursing homes, and the poor. No one ever questioned Nagin about how he spent 20 million in DHS preparedness funds, or about any of the dubious decisions he made during the disaster. Instead, the media heaped blame on FEMA mainly because they knew their criticism would go unopposed by the agency.

We all recall pictures of people hanging out of windows, stranded on rooftops, or herded into the Superdome without security, water, food, or sanitation. What one needs to know is responding to and fixing this turmoil was not FEMA's responsibility. Few realize that FEMA is no more than a support agency, whose role is pay for services obtained and controlled by state governments.

Notice I did not say FEMA provides services. To believe they alone could cure the ills of Louisiana's dysfunctional preparedness system is as ludicrous as believing Fannie Mae can fix the mortgage crisis. News flash... There is no such thing as a FEMA security guard, nurse, water company, food depository, helicopter bus company, or search-and-rescue team. All these are services paid for, not owned by FEMA. So where was the federal support in New Orleans? FEMA representatives met with Mayor Nagin and Governor Blanco more than a week before Katrina made landfall. They scratched their heads in frustration at the indecisiveness and incompetence of the people who were supposed to be in charge. Although no one will ever admit it publicly, FEMA officials became handcuffed by the inaction of local decision makers and stifled by confusion at every level.

Lack of services at the Superdome resulted from a failure by the state to submit requests to FEMA before it was too late. FEMA officials stood by, hoping the Mayor and Governor would heed their advice and warnings about evacuation, but were powerless to do anything.

They had to accept the casual attitude of Nagin and Blanco, despite the dire predictions of weather forecasters. Nagin already knew the Superdome would be the shelter of last resort for stranded poor people, well before the storm. When R&B singer Kanye West made his infamous "President Bush does not like black people" statement, the remark showcased West's ignorance of the real issues. The statement also collected support from other uninformed people who shook their fists approvingly, eager to blame anyone but the mayor for the fiasco in New Orleans.

This author is under no delusion that Mr. Bush's domestic policies were particularly advantageous to the plight of minorities or the poor. However, in fairness, Bush guided the country through the worst domestic crisis since Pearl Harbor on September 11th, 2001. He also did a credible job of managing the Katrina rescue once the magnitude of the catastrophe became apparent. The underlying insinuation of Kanye's statement was that Bush took care of whites in Florida (where his brother Jeb was Governor), but did nothing for the poor, black folks in Louisiana. Well, here is a revelation; Bush and FEMA followed the letter of the Stafford Act in administering aid to victims of Katrina. The actual reason Florida successfully managed four consecutive hurricanes in 2004 (Charlie, Francis, Ivan, and Jeanne) is because the state arguably maintains one of the best emergency management systems in the nation.

FEMA Administrator Craig Fugate is widely acknowledged as one of the most capable emergency managers in the world. It is no coincidence that Fugate was Florida's Emergency Management Director during Katrina. It is also notable that Fugate is only the second highly experienced emergency manager to ever lead FEMA. The first, James Lee Witt, served during the Clinton administration, and was credited with transforming the agency into the modern era of disaster response. Others holding the position had no background or qualifications to lead the agency, and were hired based as payback for political favors.

Despite his inexperience FEMA Director Mike Brown actually did a fairly competent job. Recall the chaos when 11,000 additional evacuees gathered at the Convention Center, begging for assistance. The center, a last minute evacuation site, is one that FEMA was supposedly unaware of until days after the storm. Unfortunately, because of the unspoken rule within FEMA that the agency cannot be viewed disparaging the state or local government, Brown pleaded ignorant, despite the fact he knew full well the catastrophe had escalated and would only get worse.

Two days after he was fired, Brown admitted in a national TV interview that he lied when he claimed FEMA was unaware of the people stranded at the Convention Center. Brown's statement made FEMA appear incompetent. This was a deliberate move by the Bush administration to deflect scrutiny from the real culprits, Nagin, and Blanco. Behind the scenes, the collective ineptitude of the mayor and governor appalled FEMA officials and stifled the efforts of Louisiana's local emergency managers. The latter were courageous souls who were doing their best to manage the local issues and protect their citizens, without any real leadership from the state.

Despite the efforts of first responders and FEMA, poor leadership caused the failures in the Katrina response, pure and simple. The media continued to malign FEMA's response while Bush, bowing to pressure, satisfied his critics by beheading the "villain" Brown. This happened after Bush had publicly praised Brown upon arrival in New Orleans. In an embarrassing twist, Bush was overheard heard saying "you're doing a heckuva job Brownie", only to dismiss him 24 hours later. With Brown firmly under the bus, Bush focused on convincing Blanco she must activate the Louisiana National Guard before he could deploy federal troops. (See U.S. Constitution).

To aid in the rescue, the Louisiana National Guard should have already been fully activated from the outset of the crisis. Blanco's alleged reason for not calling up the Guard was supposedly because many of them were deployed in the Persian Gulf. She also claimed that 4,000 troops, who remained in the state, had become victims of post-hurricane flooding (a reasonable assumption under the circumstances). Blanco further rationalized her inaction by stating she did not want to inconvenience Guard troops by activating them for rescue operations. My feelings about

Blanco's failure to protect the people at the Superdome are unfit to print. Having served a 23-year military career (19 in the National Guard), this author can firmly attest to the fact that no Guardsman would have hesitated to respond, regardless of the situation. On numerous occasions throughout my military career, I was duty-bound to leave my own family to respond to the call to help others. Leaving family gatherings, and personal crises, to serve the people of Illinois was routine. Every Guardsman and first responder understands the selfless sacrifice required of the profession, something Blanco failed to grasp.

Allow me to further clarify the misleading perception that FEMA was to blame for the poor response to Katrina. In 2004 I was assigned to oversee deployment of FEMA Community Relations teams in Alabama for Hurricane Ivan. As such, I was the lone FEMA Community Relations representative in Alabama before Ivan made landfall. Several of my counterparts were similarly assigned in Mississippi, Louisiana, and Georgia during the Ivan response. Two days before Ivan made landfall, I met state officials to discuss their response plan. The day after landfall, equipped with a FEMA credit card and the authority of the Stafford Act, I began to implement the state's plan. Several hundred FEMA community relations workers, who had arrived by chartered bus from Atlanta, had to be provided with meals, hotels, and rental cars, as well as cash per-diem. The group consisted of Citizen Corps and federal agency volunteers from throughout the country. In the coming weeks more would be deployed to set up disaster recovery centers, and perform outreach in a dozen counties. Using the Incident Command System (ICS), I was able to organize and direct the entire deployment process, with a small staff, of 3 people, from a hotel meeting room. For those who are unfamiliar with ICS, it is a command and management best practice instituted by Homeland Security in 2003. It provides a structure for managing large and small incidents. ICS provided me with a foundation to organize and manage the deployment operation. ICS is a model for organizing operations, planning, logistical support, and administration. Each position is staffed based on the needs of the incident, allowing flexibility to expand or downsize the operation quickly, without jeopardizing overall management of the incident. Use of ICS is required for all government agencies and first responders. It is a proven tool to enable a well thought-out response. Although they are not required to use ICS, many private sector and nongovernmental organizations have also adapted its methodology for managing emergencies. The point I want to emphasize is the problems during Katrina were not related to a poorly devised management structure, or lack of manpower by FEMA, as some critics alleged. The majority of the blame should have fallen squarely on the ineptitude and indecisiveness of Louisiana's top officials, Mayor Nagin and Governor Blanco. Because government first responders and officials are required to use the ICS, there is no ambiguity with regard to roles and responsibilities during a disaster operation, even one as large and complex as Katrina.

The processes of how to acquire and manage resources, organize tactical operations, and manage public information are also key aspects of the ICS model. The core failure of the Katrina fiasco started with Louisiana's top officials' inability to make good, timely decisions. To infer FEMA officials were not present or involved is a stretch of the truth at best, and an outright fabrication at worst. The fact is highly qualified FEMA managers were present and engaged a week before the storm. They could be seen standing with Blanco and Nagin at press conferences as the drama unfolded. According to some reports, Nagin was fearful of lawsuits by the business community if he ordered a mandatory evacuation of tourists in the French Quarter. Blanco's inaction for four days after the storm only deepened the crisis. Her attitude was even more perplexing than Nagin's, especially given the fact she was the principal state official. At one press conference, for example, Blanco called for prayer (always an excellent idea), but offered no other strategy as to how she intended to help thousands stranded at the Superdome and Convention Center. Meanwhile, FEMA had no authority to overturn Nagin's or Blanco's decisions. It is obvious neither of these officials understood their role. Surely, a complex disaster such as Katrina was not the time to for them to get on the job training in disaster management.

Admittedly, FEMA had its own challenges during Katrina. Critics cited the agency's slow response during the recovery. The formaldehyde infestation of temporary housing trailers provided to survivors after the rescue, created a regrettable mess for which

FEMA is fully responsible. This issue added fuel to the public perception that FEMA was less than competent. Whatever FEMA's problems, they paled in comparison to those caused by the governor and mayor. Nagin's failure to arrange the proper resources for evacuation and Blanco's refusal to activate the National Guard were negligent and deadly. As a result, the abandoned underserved were lost and turned out, and many died needlessly.

A comprehensive study of evacuees to Houston (who had stayed behind during the actual storm) found that 22% were physically unable to evacuate 14% were physically disabled, 23% stayed to care for a physically disabled person, and 25% were suffering from a chronic disease.

It was not FEMA's responsibility to make decisions regarding evacuation. FEMA can only offer advice and technical expertise to support the decisions made by the state and local governments. Despite all the bluster about the poor federal response, the truth is FEMA has positively no authority over state and local governments. The nursing home residents who drowned like rats in two New Orleans facilities should not have been there. According to New Orleans Hurricane plan, all nursing homes and hospitals were supposed to have been evacuated at least 40 hours prior to a landfall.

Ironically, Nagin drew praise from some for his tirade at President Bush. What self-respecting African-American did not want to believe they were again being victimized by the white power structure? In this author's humble opinion, many blacks were overly sympathetic to the mayor, (who coincidentally presided over one of the most corrupt city governments on the planet), simply because he was black. Nagin played the victim role to the hilt, making the talk show rounds and telling anyone who would listen how beleaguered he was at the grim situation he had tried to avoid. The fact is, in the days before the storm, Nagin sent empty Amtrak trains out of the city, failed to mobilize available school and private buses, and waited several days to call for a mandatory evacuation. All of these decisions had fatal consequences.

After the media hoopla subsided, Katrina quickly faded from the national conscience. Behind the scenes, a couple named Sal and Mabel Mangano were indicted for murder. This occurred after 35 people drowned in the nursing home they operated in St. Bernard's Parish. The Manganos became scapegoats for the inept preparation and response to the disaster. St. Rita's Nursing Home was a scene of the most horrific loss of life in Katrina. The Manganos' decision not to evacuate the home before flood waters approached outraged residents and families of the victims. Many of the deceased residents were found strapped to their beds, as water deluged the home up to its roof line.

During their trial, prosecutors claimed that three other St. Bernard nursing homes had been evacuated, and only one of their patients died. The defense to introduced evidence that most of the 60 nursing homes in Katrina's path chose to "shelter in place" as the Margano's did. For all of the misery Katrina caused and incompetent decisions surrounding it, the Manganos became the only two people to face trial. The defense contended the Manganos did their best to save the residents when the floodwaters rushed the home. Junior Rodriguez (President of the St. Bernard Parish Council), was the local official in charge, and he could have forced the Manganos to evacuate the facility. The defense argued successfully that the Manganos had safely sheltered in their brick facility for twenty years and that if the levees had not broken, the home would have been safe. The prosecution called 40 witnesses, including Governor Blanco, (who testified that she left the decision on mandatory evacuations to local officials). St. Bernard Parish never called for a mandatory evacuation.

The Manganos were ultimately acquitted of negligent homicide and cruelty charges for not evacuating the facility as the storm approached. The defense was prohibited from using testimony or documents showing the majority of nursing homes in the path of the storm, 36 of 57 did not evacuate, or that there were deaths at other homes. In one, Lafon Nursing Home in New Orleans, 22 people died. No criminal charges have been filed in those deaths. Residents were moved to the second floor as flooding began, but the home lost electricity. Rescuers did not arrive at Lafon until days later amid a heat wave that had gripped the city.

The prosecution, however, did show that three other nursing homes in St. Bernard evacuated. The Manganos were the only people in Louisiana to face criminal charges stemming directly from Hurricane Katrina, and jurors said later this played a key role in their decision to find them not guilty.

The only other criminal charges connected to Katrina deaths were brought against six former or current New Orleans police officers who faced murder or attempted murder counts from a shooting after the storm, and were subsequently convicted. The case was not connected to flooding or a direct impact of Katrina. At one time, the District Attorney's office said investigations into patient deaths at nursing homes and hospitals during and after Katrina would likely result in more arrests. Authorities investigated six hospitals and 13 nursing homes in Louisiana. At least 140 patients died in the storm and its aftermath. No fewer than 34 people died at Memorial Medical Center after the hurricane. Three women arrested by the attorney general's office did not stand trial. A grand jury refused to indict Dr. Anna Pou. The state dropped charges against nurses Lori Budo and Cheri Landry.

According to Louisiana's hurricane evacuation plan, local governments in areas along and near the coast are to evacuate in three phases, starting with the immediate coast 50 hours before the start of tropical storm force winds. Persons in areas designated Phase II should begin evacuating 40 hours before the onset of tropical storm winds and those in Phase III areas (including New Orleans) were to evacuate 30 hours before the start of storm winds. Many private caregiving facilities relied on bus companies and ambulance services for evacuation. When the storm came, they were unable to evacuate their patients because they waited too late. Louisiana's Emergency Operations Plan Supplement 1C (Part II, section II paragraph D) calls for the use of school and other public buses in evacuations.

Although buses that later flooded were available to transport those dependent upon public transportation, not enough bus drivers were available to drive them. Governor Blanco did not sign an emergency waiver to allow any licensed driver to transport evacuees on school buses. Some estimates claimed that 80% of the 1.3 million residents of the greater New Orleans metropolitan area evacuated, leaving behind substantially fewer people than remained in the city during the Hurricane Ivan evacuation in 2004.

During a panel discussion on disaster preparedness, General Honoré said, "I would not put my life on the line behind any levee". Construction and maintenance of most of the levees surrounding New Orleans is the responsibility of the Army Corps of Engineers. The storm which came as no surprise to local officials overmatched the levees. Evacuation was the only viable option given dire weather predictions of a direct hit on the city. The abyss in New Orleans became the flooding rather than the storm surge itself. Its effect was equivalent to pouring five gallons of water into a shallow one gallon bowl. The fact that the levees did not hold, however, became a secondary issue. Lack of execution of the evacuation plan took center stage in the post-Katrina blame game.

The misinformation regarding FEMA's role began early in the crisis. Louisiana officials already knew as many as 100,000 people would not be able to evacuate in time, especially given Nagin and Blanco's indecision. City officials did not implement the evacuation plan despite FEMA's repeated urgings in the days before landfall. What happens if a doctor prescribes a patient to take two high blood pressure pills a day, and the patient only takes one? If the result is a heart attack or stroke, is the doctor negligent because of his inability to control one's free will? The debate concerning who was responsible for the deaths of nearly 2,000 people in Katrina may never be resolved. Whichever version of the events one chooses to believe, an inescapable fact remains.....the citizens of New Orleans were not prepared.

CHAPTER 4

HOW UNPREPARED ARE WE?

"And God remembered Noah, and every living thing and all the cattle that were with him in the ark; and God made a wind to pass over the earth, and the waters assuaged".

Genesis 8:1

More than a decade after the tragic events of September 11, America is in many respects a different country. Enhancing preparedness and security at home, and actions to fight terrorism abroad account for significant portions of the federal budget. Under the American Preparedness Project, which tracked attitudes on domestic preparedness and terrorism over the last ten years, the National Center for Disaster Preparedness (NCDP) at Columbia University's Mailman School of Public Health recently surveyed the U.S. population. The survey made an effort to determine their current attitudes and behaviors regarding disaster preparedness and the prospect of domestic terrorism. NCDP and the Children's Health Fund conducted this survey annually from 2002 to 2008. As in prior years, the Marist Institute for Public Opinion (MIPO) executed a survey designed by NCDP and CHF. In 2011, the survey included a mix of previously-asked questions and new questions inspired by recent world events. Trended questions asked about confidence in government; extent of personal and family preparedness; and perceptions of community preparedness. The following is a summary of findings from the survey of 1,000 adults.

Citizen Preparedness

Since inception, the surveys inquired about both community level and individual preparedness to deal with the aftermath of a disaster. People were asked about their communities' and schools' response and evacuation plans, and about their own family emergency plans.

* Less than half of American feels that their community maintains an adequate response plan for a disaster that gave no warning, such as an earthquake or a terrorist event.

* Since 2003, the proportion of families lacking an emergency preparedness plan declined from nearly two thirds, but one half of American families still have no plan and 30% of those with plans still lack a critical item such as a flashlight or emergency food and water.

* Likewise, although the proportion of parents unfamiliar with the emergency and evacuation plans at their kids' schools has come down from 45% four years ago, still more than a third does not know how their schools would be handling their children in an emergency.

* Latino respondents lag behind other racial and ethnic groups on all measures of family preparedness in the survey. Respondents were asked whether the killing of Osama Bin Laden made a terrorist attack in the United States more or less likely. In the light

of the March nuclear power plant accident in Japan, they were also asked for the first time if terrorists are more or less likely to attack nuclear power plants than other targets.

* Half of Americans seem to think that the death of Osama Bin Laden will not affect the likelihood of another terrorist attack in the United States, one third are worried it will increase the chance of another attack and one sixth believe that Bin Laden's death makes another attack less likely.

* Only one quarter of Americans think that nuclear power plants are more attractive terrorist targets than other kinds of facilities.

* Black Americans are more concerned than other groups that Bin Laden's death will lead to more terrorism in the U.S. They believe that terrorists will find nuclear power plants more attractive targets.

Despite these somewhat encouraging trends, marginalized groups, the poor, and minorities suffer disproportionately in disasters. Inequities are more evident during the response and recovery stages. A thesis, entitled 'Perceived Preparedness and Preparedness Behavior for Terrorism and Natural Disasters among Low-Income African-Americans in Maryland', by Myrtle Evans-Holland, supports that argument. Although there are differences in disaster preparation behaviors between majority and minority ethnic populations, minority populations experience the inequities because of low incomes and other limited resources needed to lessen the impact of a disaster. Furthermore, scientific knowledge about differences in disaster preparedness behavior within racial/ethnic groups is limited. To address the limitation, this study was conducted among a subsample of 219 low-income African-Americans in four communities in Maryland to examine the association between perceived preparedness and preparedness behaviors. Their method studied outcomes for those having a family emergency plan (FEP) and having survival kit items (SKI) in preparation for natural disasters and terrorism. Internet access and social support were examined to determine if they caused the association between perceived preparedness and preparedness behavior to vary.

Secondary data collected by Morgan State University School of Community Health and Policy, 2006 Special Population Public Health Emergency Preparedness Initiative, were analyzed in 2008. Adults aged 18 and older completed surveys between July 31 and August 30, 2006. A statistically significant independent association between perceived preparedness and having an FEP emerged in the analysis. After adjusting for age, gender, education, employment, and Internet access, participants who perceived they were prepared were 5.8 times more likely to keep a FEP. Internet access and social support did not modify the association between perceived preparedness and having an FEP. Researchers observed an association between perceived preparedness and having more SKIS. After adjustment for age and education, participants who were prepared were 6.5 times more likely to have more SKI than those who were unprepared. However, Internet access did modify the association between perceived preparedness and having more SKIS. Social support did not modify the association.

The results from this study could be used to develop educational preparedness programs or to design appropriate interventions for underserved populations. These factors will facilitate public health emergency preparedness practitioners and researchers' ability to develop disaster education programs. It will also inform interventions to prepare those who are vulnerable and at greater risk for natural disasters and terrorist attacks. Furthermore, efforts aimed toward those at greater risk may address the disparities often seen in the aftermath of disasters particularly among low-income African-Americans in the response and recovery stages.

The results will also be useful to public health emergency planners at federal, state, and local levels and may lead to stronger preparedness actions, which will ultimately lead to greater and more effective response and recovery capabilities in the aftermath of a disaster. Other investigators found research and interventions that address the particular needs of a community may be more useful to both public health emergency practitioners and citizens.

In 2006 Young and Rubicon conducted a preparedness study for the American Red Cross. The study revealed some startling statistics about unpreparedness in some segments of the community.

SENIOR COMMUNITY AGES 75 AND UP, RETIRED, FIXED INCOME

They are not prepared:
• 93% do not have a set place to meet in the event of a catastrophic disaster
• 96% have not been certified in either First Aid or CPR in the last 3 years

They are likely to act:
• 65% will read literature to obtain additional information
• 73% would share information with their neighbors
• 37% will attend an information session
• 45% would build a kit

They might not be as prepared as they would like to be because:
• 48% do not know where to get information
• 76% have not been contacted on how to prepare

FAMILIES HOUSEHOLDS 3+, AGES 25-54, EMPLOYED AT LEAST PART-TIME

They are not prepared:
• 86% do not have a set place to meet in the event of a catastrophic disaster
• 87% have not been provided information about evacuation by their child's school

They are likely to act:
• 76% would make a plan to reconnect
• 50% will read literature to obtain additional information
• 55% would visit a Website to obtain information
• 50% would build a kit
• 43.6% have been certified in either CPR or both first aid and CPR

They might not be as prepared as they would like to be because:
• 48% do not know where to get information
• 45% have not been contacted on how to prepare

HISPANIC COMMUNITY AGES 35-54, SINGLE, MARRIED & W/CHILDREN

A significant part of the population:
• Almost 30% of the population is Hispanic or Latino

They are not prepared:
• 64% have not been certified in either First Aid or CPR in the last 3 years
• 75% have not been provided with information regarding their child's school or daycare's disaster or emergency plan
• 82% have not received information from their work place

They are likely to act:
• 30% already have a designated place to meet in the event of a catastrophic disaster
• 37% would attend an information session
• 45% would learn a life -saving skill
• 65% would build a kit
• 80% would make a plan of action to reconnect with their family in the event of a disaster

National findings of the study are likely to hold true for minorities as well:

• People 65 or older are significantly less prepared than younger Americans

• Those with an education level below a high school diploma, or a household income less than $40,000 are less prepared

• Hispanics are less prepared than whites or African-Americans

• Individual employment status and having school aged children are strong influencers on higher levels of preparedness.

• Public awareness of local disaster plans is a surprisingly low 38%

Given these benchmarks, one must overlay social factors such as education, poverty, age, unemployment, and awareness of local programs that paint an even bleaker picture of where the African-American community is with regard to preparedness.

It is no wonder that the specter of another Katrina is not only a reality, but a probability. We do not know for certain the cause or location of the next catastrophe. The uncertainty and unpredictability of natural and man-made disasters is the reason preparedness should be of paramount concern to everyone. Unfortunately, the overall picture shows we have not improved significantly in preparedness and in many respects are less prepared today than we were seven years ago during Katrina.

Nursing Homes Still Not Prepared

A Government report issued by the Department of Health and Human Services Office of the Inspector General in April 2012 shows nursing homes are woefully unprepared to protect frail residents in a natural disaster. According to the report, emergency plans required by the government often lack steps such as coordinating with local authorities, notifying relatives or even pinning name tags and medication lists to residents in an evacuation. These findings render the plans virtually useless.

Seven years after Hurricane Katrina's devastation of New Orleans exposed the vulnerability of nursing homes, serious shortcomings persist. Investigators from the inspector general's office of the Health and Human Services Department report that they identified many of the same gaps in nursing home preparedness and response.

The report points out most emergency plans lacked relevant information. Nursing homes faced challenges with unreliable transportation contracts, lack of collaboration with local emergency management, and residents who developed health problems". The report recommends Medicare and Medicaid add emergency planning and training steps to the existing federal rules requiring nursing homes to have a disaster plan. Investigators found a disregard for many steps now contained in nonbinding federal guidelines. In a written response, Medicare chief Marilyn Tavenner agreed with the recommendation, but gave no timetable for carrying it out.

CHAPTER 5

UNDERSTANDING THE DISASTER SYSTEM

"If We Had A Terrorist Attack, The Way The People Respond Is Going To Determine Whether That Attack Is Just A Tragedy, Or Whether That Attack Becomes An All-Out Disaster."

Patrick J. Kennedy

Following the creation of the Department of Homeland Security (DHS) in 2002, DHS created organizations such as Citizen Corps to facilitate local community presence and participation in disaster preparedness, response, and recovery activities. DHS established and funded Citizen Corps Councils through state grants set aside for this purpose. Most Citizen Corps Councils operate in small towns and suburbs, but many exist in larger cities. They provide training in emergency management for average citizens, conduct exercises, and serve as a bridge to local law enforcement, public safety, fire, and emergency medical services. Community Emergency Response Teams (C.E.R.T) teams learn skills to augment first responders during emergencies and nonemergency events, providing management, traffic control, communications, and other essential services. Citizen Corps volunteers participate in DHS training (provided free) in disaster management, response, preparedness, and many other aspects of training and exercises. Citizen Corps councils exist in every state, and new councils are eligible to receive an annual grant to help them operate. Levels of participation in Citizen Corps Councils by ethnic groups are unknown. The FEMA Community Preparedness Division does not track participation by demographic characteristics. In addition to Citizen Corps, other free programs are available to help families become more prepared. The Resource Guide in the back this book contains a more comprehensive listing of other preparedness organizations.

The disaster response system is fairly straight-forward. First, one needs to understand that all disasters are local events. Despite how large or unruly a disaster may become, protecting lives and property of citizens is a local matter. When an incident surpasses the ability of local governments to respond, they appeal to the county government for assistance. County assistance may take the form of equipment, people, goods and services, or a combination of those resources.

After counties deplete their existing resources, they must appeal to the State or neighboring counties for additional assistance. Many counties have Memoranda of Understanding (MOU) agreements in place to account for resource contingencies in an emergency. Some states have disaster funds to use in emergencies, however, most do not. The state may also loan resources to counties through MOUs. These agreements may be made with or without provision for reimbursement. For federal assistance, there is typically a 75% federal and 25% state match of funds required.

The Emergency Management Assistance Compact (EMAC) offers assistance during governor-declared states of emergency through a responsive, straightforward system that allows states to send personnel, equipment, and commodities to help disaster relief efforts in other states. All 50 states participate in EMAC. Compensation for resources is guaranteed by governance under EMAC, to prevent disputes between states attempting to recover expenditures.

FEMA Declarations Process

Unknown to most, a FEMA disaster declaration is not just a matter of the President deciding indiscriminately to provide federal funding. A number of rules and requirements must be met in order to receive federal assistance. Under a law, known as the Robert T. Stafford Act, there are several categories of assistance the President can approve, and some or all may be eligible for approval on a county-by-county basis depending on the scope of the disaster.

Despite the complaints of state and local politicians when they do not receive a FEMA declaration, each understands it is not a matter of the President one-sidedly approving federal aid, if the disaster qualifies under Stafford Act rules.

Unfortunately, many in the media choose to report disaster

declarations as an entitlement, making it appear as if the victims of the disaster are being further wronged by FEMA if federal funds are not forthcoming. Neither the media nor politicians bother to explain to the public, the reason federal assistance was not rendered. The typical reason a state does not receive assistance from FEMA is because they simply do not qualify. In other instances, sloppy and inadequate damage assessments, poor records management, and incomplete application data could result in not receiving a FEMA declaration. Stafford Act rules are designed to ensure fairness to communities and taxpayers alike. For example, if a community has a large percentage of homeowners with insurance, it may not qualify for certain programs. Programs are administered by county, regardless of the number of people affected in a given location. When approved, FEMA programs apply to all residents of the county, regardless of individual damages.

States, and by extension local governments, have a legal obligation to take care of their citizens. Their unwillingness or inability to take responsibility for disaster relief is reprehensible and negligent in this author's opinion. The fact remains most states have no funds set aside for disasters; hence, their only recourse for helping citizens recover is if damages are severe enough to meet the standard for federal aid.

Often the result of this political and fiscal gamesmanship has the direst consequences for the poor and underserved. Before a disaster is declared, FEMA makes every effort to help the states prepare the required paperwork for a declaration, offering technical assistance and resources needed to perform initial damage assessments. Thus, if a declaration request is not granted, it truly does not qualify, and this often sparks the ire of politicians and starts the public relations spin game. A blatant example of this "blame the feds" practice happened when this author worked at FEMA. At the time, (now imprisoned) former Illinois Governor Rod Blagojevich flew all over the state, complaining to the media FEMA had failed to help local governments recoup costs incurred fighting floods along the DesPlaines River.

The governor's public ranting continued for weeks, all while FEMA remained silent. When a Chicago Tribune reporter cornered me to confirm whether the Governor had ever requested federal aid, it forced me to admit no such request had been made. As I took the train to work the following morning, an article in the Chicago Tribune shouted the truth. *"Suburbs not likely to get U.S. flood aid"*. When I walked into the office, the outraged Governor and other state officials were already on the phone with my superiors, demanding my firing. From the beginning, Blago knew damages and expenses incurred by towns along the DesPlaines were millions short of the qualifying threshold. This was the precise reason a declaration request was never submitted to FEMA. Although my bosses supported me despite enormous pressure, the message was clear; I had violated the rule of silence and forced the state to admit to Blago's deceitful posturing.

Current Illinois Governor Pat Quinn and other state politicians recently leveled similar public criticism at FEMA, following a deadly tornado in downstate Harrisburg. This time, however, a FEMA spokesman told the media they determined Harrisburg could rebuild with assistance from state and local agencies, private insurance, and volunteer groups. Only 8% of the residents and businesses were uninsured, hence; the Harrisburg tornado did not qualify under the Stafford Act rules.

This writer is genuinely heartbroken by the devastating losses of life and property caused by disasters. However, it is disingenuous for politicians to continue deflecting responsibility for their problems in disaster relief. In cases where a state clearly does not qualify for a FEMA declaration, an honest reaction is needed. Political leaders should do a better job of funding state disaster programs, and stop blaming the federal government for their fiscal problems.

An important fact to remember is that most people at or below the poverty level cannot afford homeowner's insurance. Even those who can pay monthly premiums are still underinsured. If a disaster occurs in an area where the majority of residents are uninsured or underinsured, their chances of receiving a federal declaration are greatly improved. Obtaining FEMA assistance is never assured; however, each situation is judged fairly based on the rules. After the declaration, the first step for individuals in applying for FEMA disaster assistance is to file damage claims with one's insurance company. No duplication of benefits is permitted. FEMA will not pay for expenses previously covered by homeowner's insurance.

The Robert T. Stafford Act

Robert T. Stafford Disaster Relief and Emergency Assistance Act, PL 100-707, signed into law November 23, 1988; amended the Disaster Relief Act of 1974, PL 93-288. This Act constitutes the statutory authority for most federal disaster response activities as they pertain to FEMA programs. The Stafford Act is essentially the playbook describing FEMA's operating rules and authorities. The document covers everything the agency is responsible to provide, including loans, grants, and entitlements.

The Disaster Declaration Process

Finally, if an event is so severe that it exceeds the capability of states and local government, the Governor may request federal assistance from FEMA under the Robert T. Stafford Act. This process requires states to assess costs based on damage already incurred.

To prepare for submitting a FEMA declaration request, states coordinate with counties to develop a detailed damage assessment. This documentation includes receipts and proof of any expenditure related to the disaster. States then forward the assessments and supporting documents as attachments to a letter, signed by the Governor, addressed to the FEMA Regional Administrator in their region. FEMA is divided into 10 regions covering the U.S, Puerto Rico, Guam, the U.S. Virgin Islands and the Federated Islands of Micronesia.

After the request is reviewed, the FEMA Regional Administrator forwards the request packet to FEMA HQ in Washington D.C. The President reviews and signs the formal declaration; based on the finding FEMA has sanctioned its provisions under the Stafford Act. FEMA then sends a confirmation of approval to the Governor, detailing which counties and what types of assistance is part of the declaration. This opens provisions of the Stafford Act to allow FEMA to administer funding to the state for the approved counties.

Types of Stafford Act Assistance include:

Public Assistance (PA)

This program covers the process of reimbursement to state and local governments for disaster related expenses, such as debris removal, overtime costs for fire, law enforcement, public safety, and local expenditures. It also covers some of the costs associated with repair or replacement of roads, bridges, water systems and other critical infrastructure vital to the community.

Individual Assistance (IA)

This program provides grants and assistance to individuals and households to bridge the gap for those who are uninsured or underinsured. Individual homeowners are eligible to receive assistance for their primary place of residence; however, they are not eligible for assistance to repair damage to rental property. Renters are eligible to receive assistance for some personal property. IA is administered through an individual claim filed by the affected household. Recipients may also be entitled to temporary housing, food assistance, unemployment benefits, and transportation costs related to the disaster.

Disaster Loans

Small Business Administration (SBA) loans are made available to businesses and qualified individuals needing to make significant home repairs. These loans meet standard loan and credit criteria, can provide low interest long-term assistance, and are transferable to other family members as part of the borrower's estate. SBA disaster loans of up to $200,000 are available to individual unit owners to repair or replace disaster damages not covered by insurance or other disaster programs. Individuals may also borrow up to $40,000 to replace damaged or destroyed personal property not covered by insurance, etc. Individuals may not borrow money to repair common areas that are the responsibility of the association. Provided the development will not be repaired or rebuilt, individual unit owners may apply to SBA for relocation assistance.

This means one may have eligibility for the full replacement value of your unit and your share of the common area, minus any disaster recoveries one has received, up to lending amount limits. Applicants must submit a relocation plan to SBA for approval. Should individuals choose not to participate in the rebuilding of their association and decide to relocate, they may borrow only the amount equal to their uncompensated losses. As an owner of a unit qualified as rental property, one may apply to SBA for a disaster business loan.

About Flood Insurance

For those living in a flood prone area, lack of flood insurance can be extremely costly. Nationwide, only 20% of American homes at risk for floods are covered with flood insurance. Most private insurers do not offer flood insurance. Simply put, the risk is too high for the number of potential claims; hence flooding insurability is subject to a rule called adverse selection. In certain flood-prone areas, the federal government requires flood insurance to secure mortgage loans backed by federal agencies such as the FHA and VA. However, the program has never worked as insurance, because of adverse selection. It has never priced people out of living in highly risky areas by charging an appropriate premium, instead, too few places are included in the must-insure category, and premiums are artificially low. FEMA states that approximately 50% of low flood zone risk borrowers believe they are ineligible and cannot buy flood insurance.

Incredibly, a study by an insurance industry group found that 33% of homeowners mistakenly believe floods are covered with their standard homeowners' insurance policy. In 1968, Congress established the National Flood Insurance Program (NFIP) with the passage of the National Flood Insurance Act. The NFIP is overseen by FEMA and enables property owners in participating communities to purchase insurance as protection against flood losses. As reciprocation, insured communities are subject to State and community floodplain management regulations that reduce future flood damages. Anyone residing in a community participating in the NFIP can buy flood insurance renters included. However, unless one lives in a designated floodplain, and is required to purchase flood insurance, the policy does not go into effect until 30 days after it is initially purchased. Under the program, a component called the Community Assistance Program State Supported Services Element (CAP-SSSE) provides funds to states to help communities in the NFIP ensure flood loss reduction goals are met and build community floodplain management expertise. States must provide 25% of funds for participation while FEMA covers a 75% match for all States receiving CAP-SSSE funds.

Flood Community Rating System

The objective of the Community Rating System (CRS) is to support the goals of the NFIP. To do this, the CRS provides insurance premium rate reductions to policyholders in recognition that their communities implement activities that work toward its three goals: reducing flood damage, supporting the insurance portion of the NFIP, and pursuing a broad approach to floodplain management.

Emergency Management Training and Education

Since the September 11, 2001 terrorist attack, an entire new industry has been created in the area of disaster management. Many local, state and private colleges and universities now offer degree programs in Emergency Management, Business Continuity and related fields. In addition, professional certifications at the state, national and international levels are available.

While many reputable companies offer to train in emergency management, as with any industry, there are also a few unscrupulous operators. Remember, there are no shortcuts to hard work and experience, and the emergency management field is no exception. It is advisable to check out the credentials of the company before paying for training. Be sure to research available training before committing to paid programs that could be obtained for free.

The International Association of Emergency Managers (IAEM) is the most recognized and reputable group for national certification. They offer a Certified Emergency Manager (CEM) and Associate Emergency Manager (AEM) certification that is widely recognized throughout the U.S. and abroad as the definitive credentials in the industry. The IAEM establishes, maintains, and monitors industry standards for training, experience, and education, and acts as a protector of industry standards against fraudulent or self-made "experts".

Careers opportunities in emergency management exist in government and the private sector. Federal, state and local governments are required to certify certain employees in National

Incident Manager System (NIMS). Specialties within the emergency management field include; preparedness, planning, training & exercise, response and recovery operations, terrorism, and many others. FEMA, through its Emergency Management Institute (EMI), offers free online courses in nearly every aspect of emergency management. This training is available to individuals and organizations that seek to learn more about emergency management, or want to pursue careers in the field. Some training consists of self-paced, computer based course modules while others require enrollment in classroom courses. Many of the courses provide basic requirements for entry level employment in the emergency management profession, and most have transferrable continuing education units (CEUs) that can be used toward degree programs.

State level certifications in emergency management are also available in many states and are usually administered by the state's Emergency Management Agency, Public Safety, or Homeland Security divisions. State certifications, while valuable, are often geared toward state hazard training (Florida's program would; for example, be focused more on hurricanes). The only caveat is if one decides to relocate, the new state may not recognize another state's certification, and may require additional training courses to certify.

The National Response Framework presents the guiding principles that enable all response partners to prepare for and provide a unified national response to disasters and emergencies -

from the smallest incident to the largest catastrophe. The National Response Framework establishes a comprehensive, national, all-hazards approach to domestic incident response. Part of the National Response Framework is the Homeland Security Exercise and Evaluation Program (HSEEP)

HSEEP is a set of guidelines established by DHS in 2002. HSEEP contains programs and tools for planning and conducting exercises. It used by government agencies, disaster relief, and private sector organizations, to establish exercise standards and maintain the integrity of exercise evaluation.

The Emergency Management Cycle

The emergency management cycle describes the continuous process by which we prepare for emergencies and disasters, respond to them when they occur, help people and institutions recover from them, mitigate their effects, reduce the risk of loss, and prevent disasters such as fires from occurring.

Stages of the emergency management cycle:

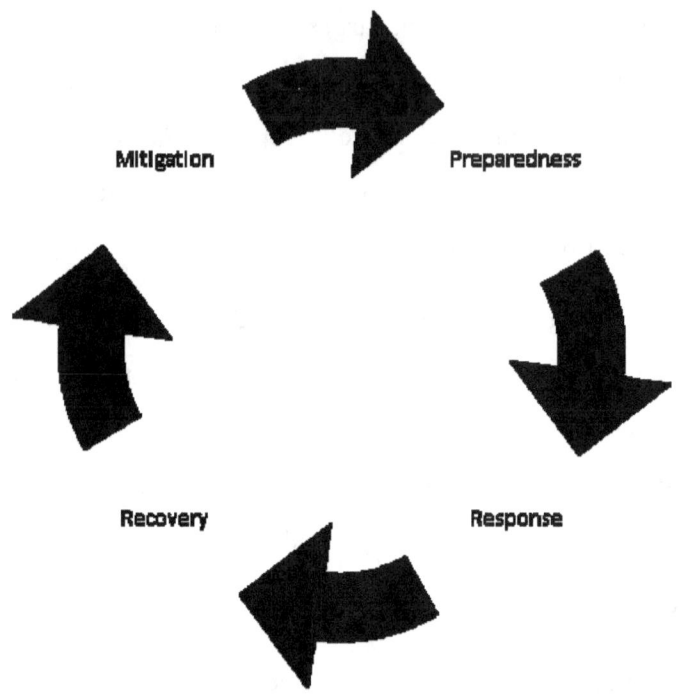

Mitigation   Preparedness

Recovery   Response

MITIGATION- Minimizing the effect of an emergency or disaster before one occurs.

Examples: building codes and zoning; vulnerability analyses; public education, smoke detectors.

PREPAREDNESS- Making arrangements for resources and planning actions to take in the event of an emergency or disaster.

Examples: family preparedness plans; emergency exercises/training; warning systems.

RESPONSE- Minimizing the impact of hazards created by an emergency or disaster.

Examples: search and rescue; emergency relief.

RECOVERY- Returning the community to normal following an emergency or disaster.

Examples: temporary housing; grants; medical care.

Far too often, the disaster cycle begins in the response phase for the underserved. Because of the gap in preparedness and mitigation, the underserved suffer more than necessary during the recovery because they have neglected the initial steps.

As a career Emergency Manager, this writer confesses to not having a disaster kit ready with equipment and supplies to sustain me for three days. What I do have, however, is a wealth of knowledge, experience, and situational awareness to rely upon if an emergency should occur. Nobody is suggesting any segment of the population should be ready to live in the woods and eat berries and leaves for a month.

It is unrealistic and impractical to believe one has the time or the resources to prepare a commando style survival kit. Being well informed and having a contingency plan for the short haul are crucial. Knowledge is power, and the more knowledge one possesses will serve to help individuals and families make smart decisions about survival when the time comes.

Mitigation Phase

Each year, FEMA spends millions of taxpayer dollars on the response and recovery phases of disasters. Of the funds allocated, 7% is set aside to perform mitigation activities. For example, if one resides on a floodplain, FEMA provides funds to local governments to buy out homes and turn the areas into wetlands, build levees, and other projects aimed at lessening the impact of future disasters in areas with repetitive losses. FEMA provides monies to the state at a 75-25 % match. It is essential to know the projects the State selects for mitigation are not directly connected to the mitigation funds received.

This means flooding in a given community does not necessarily guarantee mitigation projects will be funded to correct issues in that same community. It is essential to be informed about what mitigation projects have been designated for communities, and ensure legislators represent one's interests. FEMA requires states to have an annual mitigation plan. State emergency management web sites publish mitigation plans. They may be obtained through the state's emergency management agency.

The truth is most states have not appropriated funds for disaster relief. This is necessary to know because if a serious disaster occurs the state may be unable to fund additional relief programs. These programs are typically designed to assist citizens with unmet needs or shortfalls FEMA funds may not cover. Remember, FEMA's obligation is not to make one whole. If on is uninsured or underinsured, FEMA alone will not be able to provide compensation for certain losses. Having information about the historical and ongoing mitigation efforts in states and local communities allows one to make sound decisions to avoid repeated losses from disasters. Options may include moving, buying flood insurance, or other measures designed to protect one's family and your property. Also, understand that a FEMA disaster declaration is not automatic. A level of financial responsibility rests first with the local government, then the county and finally the state. FEMA can provide funding under the Stafford Act when all state and local resources have been exhausted.

The spirit of the Stafford Act is to provide assistance when it exceeds the capabilities of state and local government. Even in those instances, the level of financial culpability depends on the state's ability to meet its obligation to care for the needs of the public, and to provide matching funds if required. Being informed about historical risks, and managing those risks, is the essence of mitigation. Maybe it is not practical, for example, to sell one's home and move, but an investment in a truckload of sand and some sandbags may be sensible if one lives in an area where flooding is frequent.

Preparedness Phase

Whenever one walks into a restaurant, office building, or onto an airplane, make a mental note of the location of emergency exits.

This is so if something should happen and evacuation is necessary, some thought has been given to how one would escape. This is not paranoia, but a level of situational awareness we should all learn to practice. In countries like Israel, personal preparedness and awareness are a way of life. People there go about their daily lives, but rest assured they are acutely aware something can happen at any moment, and they must be prepared to survive.

Perhaps many have seen the well-crafted Homeland Security public service ads where the family sits down at the dinner table and draws a map, engages in a lengthy discussion about their disaster kit, and talks about what a fun thing it is to be ready. The reality is; few, if any, families of any economic class are going to go to any elaborate activities to prepare for disasters. What one should do, however, is to at least have a ten minute discussion in your household as to what everyone should do in an emergency. Apartment dwellers should know the location of all fire exits. Seek alternate means of escape such as a balcony or porch.

A framework for survival is established by addressing these fundamental questions. Discuss a reunification plan to get in touch with all family members if they become separated. The plan can be as straightforward as "always call grandma's house in another state" if there is an emergency. A clearly communicated plan does not have to be formal, as long as it understood by all members of the household.

Other valuable things to know and discuss with members of

your household are:

• Location of life-sustaining medication, valuable papers, documents, i.e., insurance policies

• Secure a flashlight, candles, and matches or lighter handy in case of a power outage

• Obtain a weather radio, (less than $20.00 at your local Walgreens)

• Set a supply of non-perishable food (cans) to last 2-3 days and a nonelectric can opener aside

• Keep bottled water on hand for an emergency (a case costs less than $5.00)

Taking these basic steps could change almost any emergency situation from a personal disaster to a mere inconvenience.

Response Phase

Because most of us are not first-responders (fire, police, EMS), one often wonders what they can do during the response phase of an emergency. The answer is clear. If faced with a life threatening emergency, be prepared to take the following actions:

• **Get Out** – Evacuate or escape from the immediate risk as quickly as possible. If feasible, aid others to escape danger and seek a place of safety.

• **Call Out** – Seek help by calling emergency authorities using 911 or other local response numbers.

• **Chill Out** – If one cannot escape the danger or are in its immediate path, the practical thing to do may be to shelter in place. Stay in place until help arrives rather than increase your risk of not surviving.

• **Prepare to go all Out** – In the worst case situation, whatever actions one takes may mean the difference between perishing and surviving. Be prepared to take extraordinary measures to stay alive. Taking decisive action may be your only option.

Recovery Phase

After surviving a disaster, picking up the pieces can be a long and difficult process. Help, when it does arrive, may involve red tape, long waiting periods, and multiple attempts to get back on your feet. The best advice this author can give anyone who has suffered catastrophic loss is to be calm, and realize others may be experiencing the same emotions. Seek spiritual guidance to help deal with the devastating, and often crippling emotional turmoil of the event. These mental health challenges can involve anything from injuries, to death, loss of property, employment, home, and the core elements of your way of life.

There are dozens of local, state, and national agencies ready to help in your time of need. If one survives physical injuries, he or she can begin the daunting task of rebuilding their material life. Do not be discouraged by bureaucratic red tape or delays. Be persistent, when seeking assistance one should investigate all available options. Grants, loans, and gifts are but a few of the available resources. Be patient and take things one step at a time. Issues related to recovery will take time to resolve. Feel OK about surviving the worst part of your ordeal, and be thankful to be a survivor.

Disaster Event Types

Look at the table of disaster events below, and determine which are most likely to happen in your community. Additional procedures can then be added to disaster plans to address local hazards.

<u>Natural Hazards</u>

• Winter Storm

• Hurricane

• Flood

• Tornado

• Earthquake

• Pandemic

• Severe Storm / Wind

• Drought

• Tsunami

• Wildfire

• Volcano

Technological Hazards

• Hazardous Materials Release

• Structural Failure

• Storm & Wastewater Infrastructure

• Transportation Accident

• Nuclear Incident

• Water Infrastructure

• Natural Gas Leak

Human-Caused Hazards

• Terrorism – (Explosive, Radiological, Nuclear, Biological, Chemical)

• Cyber Attack

• Civil Disturbance

• Active Shooter

• Fire (Structural)

CHAPTER 6

OVERCOMING PREPAREDNESS CHALLENGES

"All of us, but especially people in charge of a city, a theater, a business--should recognize that people can be trusted to do their best at the worst of times.
They will do even better if they are encouraged to play a significant role in their own survival before anything goes wrong".

Amanda Ripley

So why aren't we better prepared? In her book The Unthinkable: Who Survives When Disaster Strikes and Why, Time Magazine reporter Amanda Ripley, said, "only after everything goes wrong do we realize we're on our own, and the bigger the disaster the longer we will be on our own". With this in mind, the vision for preparedness must emphasize the role of the community in caring for itself. Ms. Ripley spent several years interviewing survivors of September 11 and other disasters worldwide, seeking to understand the mentality of survival. What she concluded can be summarized in absolute terms. Ms. Ripley concluded there are three basic steps in any catastrophe; shock and disbelief, realization that something terrible has occurred, and action in an attempt to survive or help others survive. The key to surviving, according to Ms. Ripley's findings, is preparedness.

Preparedness is the reason U.S. Airways pilot Chelsey "Sully" Sullenberger was able to land a jet on the Hudson River in the 2009 "Miracle on the Hudson" incident. His previous practice and training flying gliders had given him the training to succeed at landing the disabled plane. Although no such feat had ever been attempted with a commercial jet, Sully's preparedness and the quick action of his flight crew meant all 155 people aboard the plane survived.

The main purpose of Ms. Ripley's research was to demonstrate how those who survive disasters are often able to get from the "disbelief" to the "action" phase more quickly if they have had training. It explains at least in part, why some people at the World Trade Center were capable of heroic actions, while others walked around stuck in a state of dazed confusion unable to grasp the reality of their own survival. Granted there is no guarantee anyone will survive a disaster. We can, however, markedly improve one's odds of survival by having some training. If one has ever participated in a fire drill at work or school, it has significantly improved their chances of survival during an actual emergency.

To understand the lack of preparedness in underserved communities, one must recognize the historical context of the issue. After September 11, the government quickly took steps to develop the Department of Homeland Security and the National Response Plan, which would later be renamed the National Response Framework. In developing preparedness programs, the Department of Homeland Security failed to understand the core issues as to why most people, regardless of their ethnic background or economic status, are apathetic about preparedness planning. People are lazy, and also busy with the daily tasks of life connected to survival. Work, school, family, and other obligations take center stage in the lives of John and Mary Q Public. Add leisure time to the mix, and nobody wants to hear about another thing they "must" do, particularly at the cost of their two most precious commodities; time and money. Besides not having the time or money, most people also have not considered the extent to which they would be affected by a major disaster.

By 2006, the post-Katrina shock and fear had dissolved, and folks went back to business as usual. The return to normal did little to change the government's interpretation that citizen preparedness no longer required their full attention. Failure is assured if we continue repeating tired, lackluster approaches to engage people in preparedness.

The government has spent billions of dollars on preparedness since 2002, with little to show for it. The "Get a Kit, Make a Plan, Be Informed" preparedness message touted by DHS has fallen on deaf ears. Katrina did introduce the government to an untapped resource; the faith-based community, which contributed heavily to disaster relief goods and services. After Katrina, the government made several overtures toward being more inclusive of church organizations. They established the White House Office of Faith-Based Disaster Initiatives, ostensibly to provide a direct link to the religious disaster relief community.

Despite these moves, DHS remained clueless as to how churches operated, and what they could do to help faith leaders integrate into the disaster relief mainstream. Instead, in some ways they managed to further alienate the faith community because of their sometime condescending attitude, and inability to unravel bureaucratic red-tape in administering programs and training. Churches, traditionally accustomed to acting independently, remain mistrustful of engaging in government sponsored preparedness planning. Some church leaders were skeptical, fearful these alliances may undermine their own ability to administer relief programs as they saw fit. Today, churches remain uneasy about working with the government.

Many communities are unprepared because they are out of tune with the reality they are on their own, still believing someone will rescue them immediately in a catastrophe. It is not the poor and underserved communities' fault they got lulled to sleep; nonetheless this is the "new normal" of today's disaster system. In recent years, DHS and FEMA began making serious efforts designed to include the business community in preparedness planning. Once again, government may miss the boat by failing to understand the best thing they can do to help businesses recover is to get out of the way. Businesses need government help to expedite access to gain access to affected areas so they can begin rebuilding.

Current FEMA Administrator Craig Fugate clearly understands what the business community needs. After all, having dealt with hurricane recovery in Florida for years before joining FEMA, Fugate had a front row seat. He truly understands the nuances of balancing citizen protection and its connection to community recovery. Fugate's challenge is to get state and local governments to adapt a different attitude toward business recovery. Many career emergency managers still do not appreciate the true importance of the private sector in recovery. Some government responders continue to view businesses as an "additional resource" to be tapped for goods and services, when, in fact, they are the engine that drives economic resilience for the whole community.

The Government Will Take Care of Us

Hurricane Katrina should have been a wakeup call for underserved communities about preparing for disasters; however, it may have had the opposite effect. By most accounts, the public perception of what went wrong in Katrina was the failure of FEMA-- period. What we need to understand is that recent years, the game changed, and some of us failed to recognize it. In New Zealand, everyone understands the government cannot help following a disaster for a period of days or maybe weeks, depending on where they live. Admittedly, while many middle-class Americans are unprepared, the fact is they also possess better resources for coping with disasters. For instance if one has a credit card and a car, they can evacuate if necessary. For the underserved, the need to prepare is more urgent because they do not have the economic means to deal with the aftermath of a disaster by simply evacuating.

Throughout the U.S., Red Cross Disaster Assistance Teams routinely respond to residential fires every day, providing sustenance to survivors. Far too many fire victims live in underserved communities. In many instances, people die or are seriously injured, and if they do escape they often have little support after a fire. Although the efforts of the Red Cross and others are commendable, perhaps more fire deaths and injuries could be avoided if people would make it a practice to have working smoke detectors in their homes. There are free programs in almost every state that provide smoke detectors, but many homes still do not have them. Worse are instances when smoke detectors exist, but the batteries are missing or dead.

Government and nongovernment relief organizations, no matter how caring or concerned, can only do so much. After one devastating fire, I recall a survivor saying the smoke detector kept beeping, (low battery) so he took the battery out to quiet it. While we spend millions of dollars daily on goods and services in impoverished communities, little is invested in time or money on disaster preparedness. Studies have shown, for every dollar spent on preparedness we save six to nine dollars in the cost of response. Since much of that cost is passed on to taxpayers anyway, why is preparedness not given a higher priority in underserved communities? The fact remains that while, as taxpayers, we expect the government to provide services in a catastrophic emergency; some common sense and sound judgment are prudent to help avoid certain calamities. I'm not suggesting the 100,000 left behind in New Orleans could have done more to get themselves out.

For the underserved, whose only option was to walk to the Superdome, taking basic preparedness steps would have alleviated much of their suffering, and helped save lives. Actions such as packing medications for the sick, being organized to assume leadership roles, and knowing basic first aid, were sorely lacking among the survivors. These steps could not account for the shortcomings of government, but they certainly would have helped.

Underserved communities must abandon the notion that calling 911 will result in a complete resolution of their immediate problems in a disaster. Equally, the notion that if something truly significant happens, somebody is going to be there right away to save us is unrealistic in today's environment. In the best case scenario, first responders may still be delayed by the incident. Even well-equipped and capable, first responders make up only a tiny portion of the total population. The heroic acts performed at the World Trade Center by survivors were second only to those of firefighters and police officers. Without the efforts of ordinary men and women displaying courage and leadership, many more would surely have perished on that dreadful September day.

From the beginning of my emergency management career, this

author has routinely discussed preparedness issues with friends, colleagues, family, and acquaintances. The predominant response of many people I asked about their preparedness has been, "isn't that the government's problem?" Years ago, my own spouse did not view disaster preparedness as beneficial or necessary. She believed as many do that disasters are inevitable, and government alone should be responsible. While at some fundamental level underserved populations know they need to be better prepared, most people are too preoccupied with the daily tasks of life to do anything meaningful about disaster preparedness.

The Perfect Storm

In this author's opinion, Katrina represented the perfect storm of government at its worst, poverty at its worst, and classic poor decision making. More important, Katrina exposed a complete lack of citizen preparedness among the mostly poor population. Instead of passing out DVDs before Katrina, Mayor Nagin's administration should have been passing out disaster kits and training people on how to prepare for not being able to leave. Never before has a complete breakdown of the system occurred, as the one that unfolded during Katrina. Many believe had the same circumstances that occurred in Katrina taken place in a white, middle-class community; the outcome would have been decidedly different.

Assuming the government had done everything right, the fact

remains the underserved in Louisiana were not prepared to do anything to help themselves. Could it happen again? It certainly could. When we look forward toward how to correct the problems caused by unpreparedness in Katrina, and study corrective actions that need to be taken, what will ultimately matter is clear; how prepared is your community to help themselves and each other?

Hurricane Katrina displaced between 46,000 and 64,000 children according to the National Center for Disaster Preparedness. These children experience a risk factor that puts them in jeopardy for long-term poor outcomes. Making matters worse the two states which were subjects of the study, Louisiana and Mississippi, rank 49th and 50th in the U.S. for children living below the poverty level. To break through the barriers of dependency, apathy, indifference, and poverty we must ensure basic preparedness principles meld into the social fabric of underserved communities. This foundation must be built so when disaster strikes people can care for themselves and their communities. We can build a preparedness culture through education, training, public policy and a collaborative effort among all response resources.

Ethnic Barriers to Preparedness

Rich traditions of religious faith are historically part of African-American culture dating back to the early slaves. Where whites and blacks by and large differ in these beliefs, shapes how we feel about disasters. For white society, the recovery involves an attitude that getting back to normal should consume the energy of the masses. The 1886 Charleston Earthquake is the most damaging earthquake to occur in the Southeast United States and one of the largest historic shocks in Eastern North America. It damaged or destroyed many buildings in the old city of Charleston and killed 60 people. Only a few buildings in the city escaped serious damage. In the aftermath of the Charleston earthquake, public officials enlisted blacks, who had built tent cities on the outskirts of town, to remove debris and begin rebuilding.

Appalled by the spectacle of black, former slaves, who were singing, wailing, and praying in public, Whites believed the business at hand was the rebuilding effort. A vast number of blacks, on the other hand, believed the quake to be punishment from God, and got caught up in prayer and worship services which whites considered unproductive. In general, the fact of the matter is that whites and blacks think differently about many things, including disasters. A compelling example is the vast racial divide where black and white Americans wound up on opposing sides of the Rodney King police beating, and the O.J. Simpson murder trial. In the latter, many blacks believed Simpson was somehow involved, but could not make the leap from domestic violence to murder as easily as whites were. The other deal breaker in the Simpson case was the mostly black jurors' perception that police are not altogether honest. Black jurors thought it was at least possible Detective Furman could have planted the bloody glove. Whites as whole did not buy this argument, chiefly due to a lack of personal experience. In other words, having evidence planted by the cops has not happened to them or anyone they know, making it much more difficult to accept it as plausible theory.

Added to these prejudices on both sides, is a growing mistrust within the Latino community, (who coincidentally lag behind whites and blacks in disaster preparedness). The Latino population represents a growing dilemma; how does one reach people who have mistrust and misgivings about the precise institutions responsible for helping them? Many Latinos, for example, are suspicious of Homeland Security's motives behind disaster relief programs; fearing government assistance may have strings tied to Customs and Border Patrol, resulting in possible deportation for the undocumented. During the hurricanes in south Florida, FEMA Community Relations teams comprised of Spanish speaking workers were sent to neighborhoods without DHS/FEMA shirts or vehicle markings, in an effort to avoid frightening people, or forcing them to choose between getting assistance and risking possible deportation. Although laws exist to protect undocumented individuals from discrimination during FEMA disasters, this issue remains a concern for Latino populations.

Obstacles in the Faith Community

In his book, In the Wake of Disaster, Dr. Harold Koenig makes a case that the faith-based community is the solution to improving disaster mental health preparedness and response.

Because of many historical attitudes and apathy in the black church, however, an argument can be made it is also part of the problem. In a significant disaster response, the faith community, and for the most part African-American churches, has historically made a strong effort in raising money, providing goods, services, and assisting in recovery efforts. In fact, more than 2 billion dollars in relief funds and goods were reportedly raised by faith-based organizations for Katrina relief alone, with a substantial portion coming from black churches throughout the country.

Why are so few churches in underserved communities engaged in preparedness efforts? One theory is many blacks still believe disasters are inevitable acts of God, which should be treated as unavoidable consequences of God's will; therefore nothing will avoid the inevitable result of disasters.

The lack of preparedness programs in black churches is astounding. While most black churches, regardless of size, boast a devoted following of willing volunteers who will rally to support just about any worthy cause, few if any have ever had so much as a fire drill to practice evacuation of their own church building. Furthermore, churches have ministries to attend to all kinds of urgent community needs. Prison ministries, health and wellness ministries, travel ministries, and others can be found in most black churches, but few if any offer disaster preparedness programs. DHS created the office of Faith-Based Initiatives several years after Katrina in an effort to connect with the enormous power of the faith-community in disaster response. Since then, little has been accomplished in the way of changing the preparedness attitude in the faith community. Frankly, government will always have some challenges in working with FBOs. Mutual mistrust has contributed to lack of any meaningful progress toward developing effective partnerships.

Still, there is much for faith communities to learn from the public sector about preparedness and managing disasters. The same is true for the government, who can benefit from emulating FBOs skills at managing volunteers and sustaining community outreach programs. Many faith-based organizations (FBO's) lack training and information about how the disaster system works. In the African-American community, as in others, churches are often organized by theology, denomination, doctrine, and regional or national affiliation. Black unaffiliated churches hold the unique position within the FBOs. As a rule, their pastors wield enormous power and almost absolute authority to affect change within their congregations. Even though, they are excluded from the "mainstream" FBOs, this freedom affords them greater opportunity to act, unencumbered by church bureaucracy from sometimes restricting bodies that govern affiliated congregations. Pastors of independent FBOs are free to decide what, when, and how much their congregations will participate in all activities, including disaster relief and preparedness.

Dr. Koenig believes territorial disputes between various

denominations and faiths to be the greatest obstacle to bringing the FBO community together to combat unpreparedness. He maintains that too much concern about who takes the credit leads to conflict and competition among many FBOs. Critics of FBOs involvement in disaster relief cite the Red Cross' non-partisan approach as the reason they were chartered as the preeminent relief organization by Congress, rather than the religious-based Salvation Army. Quietly, some government emergency managers view FBOs as a necessary evil at best, and a Prima Donna at worst, seeing them as obstacles capable of causing problems during response and recovery.

Attitudes about the Terror Threat

Despite the ever present likelihood of a terrorist attack against the U.S., most African-American communities remain apathetic about the possibility of a terror attack. The demographics of many who perished at the World Trade Center may be surprising to those who believe terrorists choose their victims.

The victims of September 11 were overwhelmingly male (about 75 %) young (many under 40, most under 50), and white (about 75 %). About 8% were black, 9% Hispanic, and about 6% Asian. About 75% were born in the United States; the remainder came from many countries. Together New York and New Jersey accounted for about 87% of the victims. Although outraged and saddened by the loss of life at the WTC, some blacks will say privately with regard to the terror threat "they are not after us", ignoring the fact the terrorists who carried out the attacks in Washington D.C., New York, and Pennsylvania did not plot to kill Americans with an exception clause for race and ethnic origin. In fact, United Airlines flight 93 crashed by passengers who stormed the cockpit in a heroic act to thwart the hijackers, was co-piloted by an African-American.

Though it may sound ridiculous, many blacks regard terrorists as only a threat to white America, and wrongly they assume terror groups have no "personal" issues against people of color. The truth is that terrorists do not necessarily pick targets based on the ethnicity of their victims. More than 90 countries lost citizens in the attack on the World Trade Center. The foreign countries with the highest losses were the United Kingdom (including the British overseas territory of Bermuda) with 67, the Dominican Republic with 47, and India with 41. Dirty Bombs, anthrax attacks, and other acts of terror do not discriminate. Despite beliefs to the contrary, minorities are as susceptible as anyone else to cowardly acts designed to frighten us and change the American way of life. Indeed, the misfortune of being in the wrong place at the wrong time is an inevitable product of terror attacks. If one happens to be African-American and is in a store, airplane, building, or train or anywhere where a terror attack occurs, the terrorists will not offer any apologies based on the ethnicity of the victims.

Terror Risk Perceptions

Dr. Cheryl Taylor-Thompson, in her presentation at the 2007 Alpha Public Health Forum, provided some amusing quotes from African-Americans regarding terrorism threats that echo attitudes in the community. The vast majority of participants believed they were at risk for public health threats, but perceived a lower threat of bioterrorism, or terrorism in their neighborhoods.

Below are some of the typical responses made by African-Americans participating in a Baltimore survey.

Participant 1: I don't think they're (suicide bombers) gonna come to the black neighborhood...they going to go down to the rich building because they think we're nothing.

Participant 2: ....it (terrorism) actually doesn't have a color scheme. It's about where the money comes from...Madison Park Village is not where the money's at...so if you work at City Hall, and you're black then you might be in jeopardy, but not here.

Participant 3: ...I don't think they are going to come to the black neighborhoods. They gonna go for the white people neighborhoods...

Understanding Cultural Differences

The way all people handle adversity is based mostly on

personal experience, and where they fit in regard to the present circumstances. Low-income people and people of color may confront different issues, both tangible and intangible, based on their historical, as well as current experiences, and this must be taken into account in any disaster preparedness planning. Failure to do so will intensify already existing differences and increase the likelihood that tensions will be further heightened in the disaster recovery. Some of the everyday influences that must be considered in such an examination are:

• **Transportation**

Transportation out of a disaster area must be timely, supported by evacuation hubs, prepared to care for survivors immediate needs. It goes without saying people cannot leave if they do not have a means to evacuate.

• **Availability of Resources**

Resources must include information and recompense to address immediate and long-term issues. For people who rely upon monthly stipends to survive, the time of the month in which the disaster occurs will affect their ability to reconnect with sources for food, cash, and services. Additionally, reunification with family members may be an urgent need for such things as child care and elder care.

• **Recognition of Emotional Needs and Priorities**

The fact is, those who have few material possessions will be less likely to part with them easily. They may be reluctant to leave things behind that may be of no consequence to somebody with means. It will not be easy convincing them they can always "get another one" of whatever their possession may be. Furthermore, people who are unaccustomed to travel may require assistance adjusting to unfamiliar surroundings.

• Education and Communication Skills

Literacy and English Proficiency substantially affect how survivors communicate. Verbal communication and body language will provide clues as to how well people are coping, and arranging for translators and counselors at shelters may be required.

• Engaging Trusted Sources

Low-income people and people of color may be likely to feel that their interests previously have not previously been served by others, and thus may be uncommunicative or unwilling to accept direction. Depending on the level of their frustration, it may be prudent to enlist trusted individuals or institutions to work with these groups. Also, these groups are more vulnerable, and as such are often are targeted by unscrupulous people. This is another reason engagement of trusted sources is essential to provide for and protect the underserved in disaster situations.

CHAPTER 7

SOLUTIONS TO BRIDGE THE PREPAREDNESS GAP

"I beg you take courage; the brave soul can mend even disaster."

Catherine II

The whole community needs to develop a culture of preparedness. Without increased preparation, past events provide a dim view for the future. Disasters cause overwhelming fear among citizens and create increasing burdens on the resources of state and local governments and disaster relief agencies. In recent years, we have witnessed more and more state and local governments struggling to provide services in response to disasters. These difficulties are increased by the current economic climate. Many times, people expect some level of government to address recovery. Often the Federal government unfairly absorbs much of the blame when things go wrong. Disaster preparedness is everyone's responsibility. No single agency of government or volunteer organization can do it alone. Underserved communities can, and must be included to improve community preparedness by transforming the way they think and act regarding disasters.

The lack of preparedness among underserved populations can be summarized as follows:

• Historical dependency on government

- Lack of training and education about the disaster system

- Misconceptions about terrorism and natural disaster threats

- Cultural biases and taboos about natural disasters

- Lack of community leadership on preparedness issues

First and foremost, we must mobilize people to care for themselves and others. They must prepare for the disaster through training and personal plans for evacuation, shelter, food and water. Personal preparation positions one to survive a disaster and minimize the financial, physical, and emotional impact. To accomplish this, government agencies, nongovernment organizations and disaster relief agencies must collaborate to provide clearer information so that the public is better informed before the disaster. This allows individuals to evaluate the risks, options and actions they need to take to assure the safety of their families and communities.

Preparedness should be more than a passing thought or a buzzword. Each family's daily routine must include a plan for emergency supplies and basic scheme of what their household will do in an emergency. As a community, we must optimize existing resources. This includes prepositioning emergency food, water, and supplies, and establishing cross-regional networks to create redundant coverage in any sector.

Communities must learn to utilize government resources and local businesses as integral parts of their disaster response planning. Local governments and relief agencies should have pre-arranged formal or informal agreements with businesses to provide goods, services and volunteers. Businesses should be well-informed about the non-confidential aspects of response logistics and donations. Public officials and emergency managers must also begin to view underserved populations as resources rather than victims. To reinforce this effort, we must increase opportunities for individual emergency training in CPR and first-aid. Requiring teenagers to obtain first aid skills training before receiving their driver's licenses is one idea to increase preparedness. This would substantially increase the pool of trained bystanders in every community.

Disaster preparedness courses could easily be integrated into existing physical education classes in schools. Until preparedness becomes a "must do", most people are never going to find the time to get around to getting prepared. Plans and processes between faith-based organizations, health care providers, human services, first responders, relief agencies and community groups need to be streamlined and coordinated to prevent duplication of effort and wasted resources. Those who volunteer their time and talent to create resilient communities should become full partners in training and exercise efforts. Too frequently, volunteers are used as just-in-time resources, only to be cast-off after the event.

Volunteers must be prepared and trained to assist government responders in disasters. Response organizations should have plans in place to utilize spontaneous volunteers, to reduce ramp-up time for mobilizing them. The first step in creating a plan is to take bold and innovative approaches to provide leadership of preparedness within the community. A change in attitude, action, and an aggressive approach to redefine public policy is imperative to achieve this goal. The combined efforts of government, business, philanthropy, community-based groups and the faith community must be interconnected into a singular purpose; to get ready. Failure is not an option. The lives and well-being of families are at stake. Three goals must be achieved to realize this vision:

1. Develop a culture of preparedness

2. Create collaborative inter-organizational networks

3. Identify, obtain and manage assets

In an interview on National Public Radio, author Amanda Ripley (The Unthinkable) explained her theory about disasters and preparedness. She concluded all of us undergo a three-stage process when we find ourselves in moral peril: denial, deliberation and the "decisive moment," during which the survivor buckles down and acts. The key to surviving according to Ripley is to understand one's instincts, which, in a crisis, may betray us. This perspective helps us understand each person in the community must prepare to take responsibility in the event of a disaster. The first step in achieving the preparedness vision is to convince individuals to embrace the need for preparation.

Developing a Culture of Preparedness

Many factors must be considered when developing a culture of preparedness. First, we must design this preparedness culture in a manner which ensures the underserved population is prepared without being overwhelmed by fear, ignorance, or misconceptions about threats. Second, we must be sure to address the entire population, keeping those individuals with functional needs at the forefront of preparedness efforts. Third, we must ensure preparedness initiatives address all hazards. This is because response actions may vary depending on the disaster. The most crucial aspect of the vision is to make certain preparedness activities are relevant to people's daily lives. We can best address this issue by using existing linkages to integrate preparedness activities. We can create realistic training experiences by using exercises to provide meaningful inclusion of underserved populations, practicing together with first-responders and emergency managers.

Much of the behavior of survivors can be attributed to a skill or practice they learned before the actual event occurred. The truth is any training, information, or practice before something happens is preparedness at its core. Sure, it would be fantastic if everyone could afford a fully equipped survival kit. The reality though, is being well-informed is more beneficial to surviving a disaster than any amount of equipment or supplies one could ever possess. Emergency managers at all levels should give serious consideration to adding underserved populations to your multiyear training and exercise plans. All the first responder training in the world will not be enough if citizens, particularly those who are most vulnerable, are not capable of helping themselves.

Creating Collaborative Inter-organizational Networks

Building on the cultural foundation of the community established with the first goal, we must envision a future where first responders and residents in underserved communities work together seamlessly, with a common understanding of needs, roles and responsibilities. To accomplish this, we must carefully coordinate preparedness activities across responder groups to make the most efficient use of limited resources. This requires effective communication and collaboration across a network of organizations with ties to both responders and citizens in each community. A common trusted source must be identified to ensure quick resolution of issues or conflicts which could hinder the response. The trusted source may take on many forms depending on the makeup of the community. In some instances, public safety, or the local church would play a prominent role. In any case, whoever the organizations are, each must be willing to subordinate their own self-interests for the greater good. In other words, lead, follow or get out of the way.

Identifying, Obtain and Manage Assets

The first two goals address the importance of human resources both at the individual level and those of first responders. We must also be able to use technology and manage resources, such as food and water, supplies, shelter, transportation and utilities. These resources should be made available to those within the community who are most impacted by the disaster. This means needs of the underserved must be prioritized, and resources should be allocated based on their needs. While this may seem like a logical goal, the realities of how we operate in today's environment paint a vastly different picture. The fact is, had the poor communities in New Orleans been more prepared, residents would have been able to help themselves, and the danger to first responders who had to rescue them would have been considerably decreased. Despite the best efforts of everyone, disasters can, do, and will happen. Natural and man-made catastrophes are inevitable. The three goals discussed earlier represent the lens through which we can envision a positive disaster response where the whole community is prepared. Each goal includes a set of strategies which include public policy recommendations, action steps, and progress measurements. The following section highlights strategies related to each goal.

Personal Responsibility

The first step in creating a culture of preparedness is to instill a sense of personal responsibility. This entails ensuring underserved populations understand what it means to care for themselves and their loved ones during disasters. Each member of the community must develop a deeper commitment to "what am I going to do", rather than "who will come to help me". In doing this, individuals must consider adapting personal preparedness plans for incidents which could occur when they are at home, or at work. This is no easy task for those who are living at or below poverty level. Time spent doing anything but surviving is at a premium for these families. The strategy to accomplish this sense of personal preparedness must include innovative ways to increase personal training, engage the public, and drive psychological engagement.

Community

As individuals begin to feel responsible for their own actions before, during, and after an emergency, it is inevitable for them to develop a sense of responsibility toward, and empathy for, their friends and neighbors with functional needs. The strategy to accomplish this sense of a prepared community will expand individual engagement. This can be done by building a stronger sense of community, practicing diversity and inclusion, and acknowledging needs of the whole community. Preparedness can then begin to flourish within schools, the workplace, hospitals, nursing homes, and churches throughout the community. The strategy will also address ways group affiliations (e.g. faith-based organizations, social networks) can stimulate individual preparedness.

Communication

Consistent communication is a critical success factor driving a community's ability to respond to disasters. Reliable, trustworthy communication is essential, not only during the disaster, but well before it occurs. Coordinated and consistent preparedness messages should be communicated well before a threat becomes an incident. The strategy to accomplish effective public information dissemination to the community will require identifying those individuals, organizations and resources viewed as trusted sources, and ensuring a comprehensive communication plan is in place. All segments of the population should be fully informed as to the appropriate communication channels for different types of messages. The plan must include monitoring social media, and other sources to address inconsistencies or inaccuracies, control rumors, and quickly identify issues which could result in harmful influences that hamper operational realities. An example would be to have a local trusted source verify and quash a rumor about looting or other issues, or if true, communicate back to the community, law enforcement's plan to resolve the issue.

Participants are more assured when they are well informed. Poor communication with the survivors has been the Achilles heel of many disaster responses. Because disaster preparedness is often a low priority when no immediate threat is present, efforts must be made to "market" the urgency of disaster preparedness. Preparing people for potential hazards without instilling fear is important to any outreach campaign. The main goals should include educating the underserved about what will occur *after* the disaster, to instill confidence and increase cooperation.

Stakeholder Groups

Stakeholder groups include those local first responders, volunteers, and nontraditional sources such as private sector volunteers, to fill gaps in service among local groups. Some resources may come from outside the region. The strategy for coordinating these various stakeholder groups must include verifying the capabilities of each group, so planning and deployment can be well coordinated. This is the best way to ensure rapid mobilization and efficient use of resources. It also ensures the response team has broad representation to address the needs of the entire community, including those who have limited capabilities.

Coordination

Identifying stakeholder groups alone may not be not sufficient, to accomplish the vision. Groups must be familiar with each other, have clear rules of engagement, and ensure points of contact are established. In 2002 FEMA and the Department of Homeland Security established the National Incident Management System (NIMS), which is recognized as the best practice doctrine for managing disasters at all levels. Although government agencies and first responders are required to use NIMS, private sector companies, faith-based organizations, and nongovernmental relief agencies are not. It is incumbent upon the latter groups to adapt and train using NIMS. This will ensure the response effort is not hampered or delayed due to confusion, infighting, and practices that do not lend themselves to effective disaster management. By operating under NIMS structure, non-governmental groups can bring greater value during response and recovery operations, and become more "user-friendly" partners.

CHAPTER 8

THE IMPORTANT ROLE OF THE FAITH COMMUNITY

"For unto whomsoever much is given, of him shall be much required: and to whom men have committed much, of him they will ask the more."

Luke 12:48

Every Sunday morning all across America, millions of people attend church services. African-American churches are historically the most influential institution in the community. Baptist, Pentecostal, Methodist, Lutheran, Church of God in Christ, A.M.E, Catholic and non-denominational institutions, are indisputably an integral part of African-American culture. The Civil Rights movement of the 1950's and 60's was born in black churches in the Deep South. Dr. Martin Luther King's Southern Christian Leadership Conference was the anchor of social change. Several key characteristics of black churches provide some insight into how they operate, and the importance of their ability to affect change in preparedness of underserved communities.

In the black community, preaching is a strong feature of most churches. Black ministers are often charismatic speakers, who can wield immense power and influence over their congregations through sermons. Black pastors are revered, respected, and celebrated by their congregations. Their authority and influence over the affairs of church life is accepted by their members without question. Mega-church pastors like T.D. Jakes, Creflo Dollar, I.V. Hilliard, Bill Winston, and Frederick K.C. Price, oversee hundreds of thousands of followers. In smaller churches throughout America, pastors who have similar appeal in underserved communities are likewise vital to establishing successful preparedness initiatives. A word from the pulpit by the pastor can galvanize, summon, and inspire, support for preparedness in a way no government agency, politician, or social agency ever could.

Churches not only serve as the spiritual anchor for many underserved communities, but more often than not they are weaved deep into the social fabric of the community. In many black communities, for example, the church one attends defines the social structure with which they identify. Social issues like poverty, crime, drug abuse, elder care, and education are all regularly addressed in the black church. If Homeland Security begins at home, African-American churches are essential to strengthening the community's ability to prepare for and survive disasters. Disaster and emergency response planning at the local, state, and federal level reflects how poorly understood the role of churches is as a critical response resource. In minority communities particularly, the church is routinely excluded from preparedness, training and exercises. Churches are overlooked as nothing more than a resource for post-disaster fundraising or commodities in many communities.

The task of leading the preparedness effort is not the business of churches alone. Even so, given that the faith community contributes millions of dollars for disaster relief. Therefore, it is reasonable to conclude; much more could be accomplished if some church resources were channeled into preparedness activities.

Strengths of the faith community include:

1. Ability to organize and mobilize spontaneous volunteers.

2. Ability to raise money and acquire goods and services.

3. Ability to provide mass care and shelter.

4. Ability to provide leadership and influence public policy.

5. Ability to provide spiritual guidance, comfort and counseling to disaster survivors.

The important role of the faith-based community in disaster preparedness cannot be overstated. The black church, in particular, is the singular force that could exert the most influence on disaster preparedness in underserved communities. Why? Because the most significant change required is attitudes about preparedness. Of all institutions in the African-American community, the church is better positioned to bring about the attitude transformation needed to energize underserved populations.

Ironically, the African-American faith community may in some ways be partly responsible for black's inconsistency in preparing for disasters. Viewing calamities as God's will, or punishment, are long held beliefs perpetuated for generations in many black churches. Some pastors, however, take a different view. Reverend Marvin E. Wiley, Senior Pastor of Rock of Ages Baptist Church in Maywood, Illinois, reminded his congregation that the bible says worry is inconsistent, illogical, and unnecessary.

"You do not have to worry about tomorrow, for it is in God's capable hands", Wiley said. He further suggests that, as believers, we should honor God by doing the work he has given us to do. As Noah did by building the Arc, we must be obedient to God's direction, using the tools and knowledge he has provided us. We must stand strong despite criticism, and do God's work despite how futile it may appear to others.

If one trusts God to get them a job, for example, they cannot simply sit at home waiting for the phone to ring. They must go and fill out applications. In the same regard, in trusting God to help during life's disasters, one must still do their part by preparing.

What Churches Can Do To Help Families Prepare

Every time I hear about a house fire resulting in fatalities, I wonder how different the outcome may have been if the occupants of the home were better prepared. The importance of having a family discussion of what they would do in case of a fire may indeed make a difference in preventing many such tragedies. The local church is skilled and capable of providing information to the community and influencing meaningful change. Every week, thousands of pieces of information are disseminated and distributed by churches. Bulletins, electronic messages, and emails about upcoming events, seminars, activities, and events are principal methods of communication about fundamental aspects of church life. The internet only served to expand the church's ability to communicate, and many churches now have web sites to maintain communication links, the life blood of many local communities. Providing social, political, personal, and spiritual guidance to believers and nonbelievers alike, churches enjoy a unique position in many underserved communities.

These natural connections can be leveraged to get the word out about preparedness, and emphasize it as part of the church culture. The culture of preparedness we need to create will find support in the African-American faith-based community. How do we get black churches to engage in the process of preparing the community? One example of collaboration is a program known as the Illinois-Faith based Emergency Preparedness Initiative (IFBEPI). Established in 2007 during the pandemic flu scare, IFBEPI is a model for what can be accomplished through church/community participation in preparedness.

Under a program, created by the Illinois Department of Public Health, IFBEPI trained church leaders in basic disaster management and preparedness. They also provided free classes in the National Incident Management System (NIMS) and educated over 300 churches throughout Illinois on how to prepare their congregations for emergencies. Resources such as disaster kits were provided to hundreds of churches. Many churches participated in tabletop exercises alongside public health and Red Cross planners. These exercised tested the efficacy of their newly acquired knowledge and skills in a realistic disaster scenario.

The IFBEPI program issued hundreds of disaster kits and information packets to churches throughout the state in both rural and urban communities. Town hall style seminars provided at churches, and public health centers gave pastors hands-on training regarding development of church disaster preparedness programs. IFBEPI is a model that should be emulated to engage the faith community in preparedness programs. Unfortunately, due to state funding cuts the program never reached its full potential. What should faith leaders and church members do to ignite the effort to prepare their communities? Below are some suggestions for faith-based organizations to consider.

Prepare

Preparation begins by talking to your families, households, communities and congregations about how to plan for disasters. Disasters may include emergencies that your community may be susceptible to such as tornados, floods, blizzards, and terrorist attacks, or disease outbreaks. Preparation may include using checklists to organize activities, and building emergency kits or "go bags" for elderly and other vulnerable members.

Questions to help guide preparation include:

• Do you have a family emergency plan?

• Do you have a "go-bag" of emergency supplies prepared in your household?

• Do you have an emergency supply of medical equipment for those individuals with special needs (include the elderly, infants, those with disabilities, etc.)

• Do you know the phone numbers for all your family members to contact in case of an emergency?

• Do you have a backup of these phone numbers in your wallet or purse?

• Do you have an out-of-town contact to assist in reuniting with family, sending essential assistance resources, or providing a safe place for you and your family?

• Do you know who to contact during a statewide emergency?

• Do you know the phone numbers to your physician, pharmacist, medical insurance, homeowners insurance, employer, school, religious leader/organization, local Red Cross, local health department the local police department and local/area hospital?

Practice

• Does your church have a disaster preparedness ministry?

• Have you ever had an evacuation drill at the church? If not, use the end of service when people are already departing to practice an evacuation of the building.

• Act upon your plans. Practice and build upon them. Organize with your communities and congregation family to exercise your plan.

• Build relationships within the local community emergency management agency.

• Check expiration of your emergency kits and rotate your supplies in needed. Customize supplies to better fit the needs of your church members and communities.

• Make sure all seniors and people with functional needs and disabilities have a personal kit and plan in the home for emergencies.

• Take a CPR course through the local health department, community organization, the local chapter of the American Red Cross (http://www.redcross.org). Locate CPR first aid trained members of your congregation, and enlist them to teach a class.

• Join your Community Emergency Response Team (CERT) to learn more about disaster response skills, and be active in other emergency preparedness projects in your community

Plan

• Does your church have a continuity plan in case the church building becomes uninhabitable due to fire, flood, or other emergency? If not, create a Continuity of Operations Plan (called COOP) to prepare for:

• Continuation of church services and church business at an alternate location if necessary

• Resumption of critical church functions during an emergency, where some staff may be too sick or unable to come to work.

• Creating a system to notify members or communicate critical information.

Prioritize

Disasters can and will happen. Simple steps to prepare now may mean saving lives later and protecting your congregations, communities, families and property. Make preparedness a priority within your church, and then as your church becomes better prepared, work with others in the faith community, government, and private sector to expand your program. There are many resources available to provide guidance, information and financial assistance to help your church prepare.

Additional preparedness planning tips for faith-based organizations include:

Prepare the staff to be ready in case of a disaster.

B. Assign a disaster coordinator and alternate(s)

C. Establish clear lines of responsibility and authority

D. Prepare a continuity plan in case of the pastor's absence

E. Identify members and staff trained in CPR and first aid

F. Train ushers and deacons to respond appropriately

Make a list of your facility, resources, and assets.

List members of the congregation with special needs and plan for communication during an emergency. Be sure to include:

A) Transportation (buses, vans, automobiles, trucks)

B) Communications (radios, cell phones, automated call out systems)

C) Facilities (shelters, warehouses, food pantries, day care facilities)

D) External Resources (partnerships, affiliations, Memoranda of Understanding, contracts)

CHAPTER 9

CREATING SUSTAINABLE
PREPAREDNESS MODELS

"We need to overcome our collective denial about natural disaster, and we need to budget for it and prepare for it, and if we did, we'd have a more civil and just society."

Theodore Steinberg

The lack of support for marginalized groups in emergency preparedness is a public health issue. If we only look at Hurricane Katrina as an example, we are able to correlate the direct effect of the lack of support for the underserved. This includes disaster preparedness education and readiness skills relevant to a public health crisis. After Hurricane Katrina, many research studies were conducted. Academic studies institutions that could aid in planning for future disasters have also taken steps in the area of preparedness planning. Harvard University School of Public Health established one of the prominent research projects. They created a CDC funded research center which validated criteria and metrics for public health emergency preparedness.

The CDC believed that funding such an effort was a priority, and maintaining a center geared toward specifically adapting and following through on research projects was essential. The LAMPS Project, conducted through the School of Public Health at Harvard University, consists of two main parts. The first involves researchers investigating emergency preparedness and public health system issues. These issues were divided into smaller ongoing research projects and the results are shared in order to maintain a level of accountability and record, for the sake of informing the public as well as emergency management personnel.

The second part of the LAMPS Project involves public health working in emergency preparedness on local, state, and national levels. These public health practitioners are able to access the resources through the website as a result of numerous research studies. The state and local governments ideally implement those research studies. Often these studies are unavailable to the public. Academia continues to gain more insight into the preparedness models implemented, which is part of a trend post Katrina. The LAMPS Project website allows emergency planners, and the general public to preview existing studies, and apply them to personal disaster plans. Up-to-date information is available on CDC's Emergency Preparedness and Response website:.http://www.bt.cdc.gov/.

According to the LAMPS website, LAMPS' unique multidisciplinary team comes from leading academic, medical, and public health institutions. Team members lead four projects, each focusing on distinct areas of emergency preparedness, ranging from systems improvement and engineering systems analysis, to communications and drills/exercises. Each project follows LAMPS' four-step Measurement Development Cycle (MDC) framework.

Project 1: PHEP Systems Improvement

Project 2: Engineering Systems and Analysis

Project 3: PHEP Communications

Project 4: PHEP Drills and Exercises.

The Center's Research Core provides oversight and creates synergy between research projects, allowing researchers to create novel criteria and metrics for assessing PHEP for public health systems. In addition, the Core coordinates the efforts of the LAMPS advisory committee and supports new research investigators and pilot projects.

Some of the research projects and peer reviewed articles provide public access via the website to information that is current and includes significant data and research. However, for the public there are a few articles and aspects of the website that are more relevant to daily emergencies than others. Public Health Emergency Preparedness at the Local Level: Results of a National Survey is a powerful article describing how emergency preparedness looks based on a survey. It is recommended local emergency managers and others interested in understanding how to develop and measure progress in community preparedness, read the article.

Using existing public health models, coupled with innovative programs, we can create a preparedness culture that is truly sustainable.

The Chicago Metropolitan Agency for Planning (CMAP) Go to 2040 Project is another noteworthy preparedness initiative this author had the privileged of leading in 2009. The project was part of a long-range planning effort commissioned by the Chicago Community Trust (The Trust) and the Chicago Metropolitan Agency for Planning (CMAP) covering key regional issues.

- Economic development

- Human and Community Development

- Environment

- Land use

- Housing

- Transportation

The American Red Cross of Greater Chicago, where I served as Regional Preparedness Manager, was tasked to develop a report detailing current conditions, key issues and recommendations for actions to improve emergency preparedness in the Chicago metropolitan region. This author was privileged to lead an advisory committee consisting of key stakeholders who assisted in developing content for the report. The committee consisted of stakeholders from government, business, philanthropy, non-profit, human services and community based groups from throughout the region. The advisory committee donated their time and expertise to assist in a collaborative, ground-breaking endeavor. The result of this year long project was the Chicago Regional Planning Report –

Analysis and Recommendations on Emergency Preparedness. The Red Cross submitted the report to CMAP and The Trust in May, 2009. It includes key indicators to be used to measure the Region's progress year-by-year over the next thirty years. It also contains recommendations for public policy actions to strengthen emergency preparedness today and in the future.

The key indicators to be measured include:

• Citizen Preparedness

• Municipal All Hazard Plans Capacity

• Mass Care Capacity

• Emergency Responder Communications

• All-Hazards Plan for special needs populations

• Animal Evaluation

• All Hazard Early Warning

• Medical Evaluation

• Disaster Survivor Outcomes

• Business Community

• Public Building / Institutional All Hazard Plans

The CMAP Emergency Preparedness Report contains specific and detailed phases for accomplishing many of the preparedness goals I have discussed in previous chapters. Another illustration of how to build a preparedness culture is to implement the types of training needed to accomplish the vision.

A program called Save-A-Life, started in 2003, is an example of one preparedness training concept that worked. The Save-A-Life Foundation (SALF) was created by a suburban Chicago mother named Carol Spizzirri, to teach youth to perform life-sustaining first aid skills. Ms. Spizzirri started the foundation at the urging of Dr. Peter Safar (founder of the American Heart Association) and Dr. Henry Heimlich (Heimlich maneuver), after her 18-year-old daughter Christina was killed in a roll-over auto accident. EMT's responding to the accident were allegedly untrained in basic first aid, and failed to stop Christina's bleeding, resulting in her death according to reports. Although the circumstances of Christina Spizzirri's death were unclear, the result of this tragedy exposed a glaring weakness in Illinois' EMT training system.

Unknown to most people at the time of the incident, Illinois law did not require first responders to certify in basic first aid training. Spizzirri changed this by lobbying the Illinois legislature for a change in state law. The result was the passage of a bill requiring all fire, police and EMS to receive life-sustaining first aid skills training, and to complete annual refresher courses. Most Illinois EMS organizations welcomed the law because it was another step toward improving their profession's standards; however, it was not well received by police departments, many of whom believed they were being "forced" to administer first aid.

Indeed, some departments and sought ways to get around the training requirement, to act out their displeasure with the mandate.

While some police organizations publicly praised SALF's efforts to train children, privately they scoffed at the notion they were responsible for giving first aid, despite protection by Good Samaritan laws. Spizzirri ignored her critics and persevered. By 2005, SALF had trained more than a million public school children in age-appropriate first aid courses, with testing and skill retention verification conducted 90 days and 6 months after the training. The premise of SALF training was brilliant in its simplicity. Paramedics, EMT's, and firefighters from local communities would volunteer to go into local schools, using the SALF materials to train children in basic CPR and first aid. Small government grants and private donations funded the program. Funds were used to provide mannequins, books, and testing cards. The program also provided volunteer instructors a $1.00 stipend per child trained, to cover costs of local travel to and from the schools.

Over time, SALF assembled some high-profile donors and sponsors including NASCAR, and actor David Hasslehoff, who did public service announcements on behalf of the foundation. Provided at no cost to the schools, SALF required minimal classroom time (average one hour per class per year). Schools also appreciated SALF's reinforcement of existing life-safety programs like fire prevention.

Unfortunately, SALF lost its funding in 2008 and is now

defunct. The organization's demise was due in part to a negative "investigative report" by a Chicago television station. Spizzirri needed no medical credentials to run the organization; nonetheless her failure to produce a nursing license became a lightning rod for criticism. Foundation literature and Spizzirri herself had claimed she was an RN. The report also implied SALF had not substantiated training numbers, and alleged Ms. Spizzirri's daughter did not die under the circumstances she claimed. Unproven accusations against Spizzirri and SALF so damaged the reputation of the organization that funders backed out, and forced Spizzirri to close the foundation.

Not so coincidentally, at the time of the negative media attack, SALF was on the verge of receiving substantial federal support. The additional funding would have allowed SALF to offer its program to thousands of public schools nationwide. Former Chicago Schools CEO Arnie Duncan, now U.S. Secretary of Education, provided yearly grants to the organization. SALF trained thousands of Chicago Public Schools students each year. SALF's programs demonstrated children could be trained and retain an "adult" skill like CPR. Credited with numerous confirmed accounts of children saving choking victims using the Heimlich maneuver, the training proved effective. The SALF experience also demonstrated training children could contribute significantly toward creating a preparedness mindset at a minimal cost.

A monumental step toward preparing underserved

communities would be to implement a program similar to SALF in the schools. The benefits to the whole community could be measured, using public health modeling, to ensure accountability and effectiveness of the training. Divided into instruction levels, K-3rd grade, 4th-7th grade, and 8-12th grade, SALF provided graduating levels of complexity and reinforcement of previously learned skills. Over the course of a child's primary and secondary school experience, they would be guaranteed to master these basic lifetime skills. Like swimming, CPR and first aid are skills that may only be used occasionally. The overarching goal of SALF was to increase the pool of trained bystanders, who are more often than not the critical link in the chain of survival.

In Seattle Washington, a program to teach CPR to individuals who work with the public such as cab drivers, bus drivers, retail store employees, and public transit staff, delivery personnel, mail carriers, messengers, and others has existed for more than 30 years. The Seattle Fire Department's Medic II Program provides training classes in CPR and choking techniques. Recognized as an international model, Medic II has attracted worldwide acclaim. People from around the world, have inquired about the program, and many go to Seattle to learn more about how to implement their CPR training programs. Since Medic II began in 1971, over 817,500 Seattle/King County residents were and retrained in the lifesaving technique of CPR. Studies have shown that prompt bystander CPR more than doubles a patient's chances of becoming a long-term survivor. Firefighters conduct classes on their own time, and are compensated from a donated budget. They train 10-12,000 Seattle/King County residents annually. Medic II - CPR offers five kinds of classes:

• Adult CPR class

• Adult Refresher class

• Infant/Child CPR class which focuses on injury prevention and safety.

• AED/CPR class for groups that have purchased an Automated External Defibrillator (AED).

• ESL/CPR class that has a specially developed curriculum, which is designed to meet the needs of ESL (English as a Second Language) students, and the limited and non-English speaking populations.

The Medic II program was funded, in part, by United Way through the end of 2006. It is a donation-based organization which relies upon public support for its survival. Recently, reduced donations and increasing expenses have made the program's future uncertain. Established as a requirement for gaining employment in certain public contact professions, Medic II allows those who do not want to participate to choose other employment. The intent is that there would not be a requirement for these employees to take action in an emergency; however the goal is to ensure as many trained bystanders as possible are available.

Credited with reducing heart attack deaths by 45% since its

inception, Medic II administrators recommend those considering similar programs; thoroughly explore state Good Samaritan laws to ensure liability issues are addressed.

The Role of Government

Public health departments, because of their focus on wellness, prevention, research, and testing, are far better equipped to design and administer preparedness programs than Homeland Security and FEMA in this author's opinion. Despite their best efforts, the latter has made nary a dent in anemic citizen preparedness numbers during the seven years since Katrina, or even before. While getting a kit and making a plan are excellent concepts, the reality is people are only going to do what is easiest and least expensive. DHS has no clear answers for motivating an apathetic public to prepare. A disaster kit on every shelf is neither practical nor realistic for most people, especially the underserved. Providing billboard, radio and TV ads exhorting people to prepare has been ineffective.

Another program that deserves consideration as a preparedness model is the Illinois Faith-Based Emergency Preparedness Initiative (IFBEPI), discussed in an earlier chapter. Training churches on the nuances of the disaster system, and utilizing their facilities for local shelters, are practices that can be duplicated in any community. Tabletop exercises, town hall meetings, and seminars conducted under the IFBEPI initiative served as reinforcement of learned skills. Funding shortages have severely curtailed the activities of the program over the last several years. Effective preparedness programs must start at the grass-roots level. Governments at every level should provide technical expertise and funding to support local programs. They must also take a hands-off approach, allowing local organizations to tailor programs to the community's needs. Government funders must learn to check their ego at the door and not act like an authoritative parent, scolding local communities for not doing everything according to their specifications.

The Role of Businesses

Since 2008, FEMA and DHS have made a concerted effort to engage business in disaster preparedness planning. Led by FEMA director Craig Fugate, the agency has established robust programs to ensure resiliency of businesses, which are the life-blood of disaster recovery. As for underserved communities, these efforts will aid in rebuilding disaster stricken neighborhoods by expediting recovery. Many businesses, particularly large companies, are beginning to engage with community groups to expand outreach efforts. If there is a silver lining in the cloud of preparedness for the underserved, it is the aggressive efforts of companies like Target, Sears, Wal-Mart, Walgreens, and many others to serve disaster survivors. Local emergency planners should actively engage with businesses, large and small, not only to obtain donations, but to partner on initiatives to help underserved communities *before* a disaster.

Integrating Preparedness into Daily Activities

While all these preparedness steps sound convincing on paper, the realities of one's daily existence cannot ignore the facts:

People spend a sizeable percentage of their time performing "have to" tasks of survival such as work, caring for family, school, and associated activities. Leisure time is scarce and precious, and many of us have but a few hours each week or month to pursue non-survival activities.

While most people agree that need to prepare for emergencies is essential, taking steps to prepare is low on their list of priorities. Many want to prepare but wonder how they can find the time, or money to get ready for disasters. The solution to this dilemma, to prepare or not to prepare, is not as complex as one may think.

• At the workplace, most employers have some level of workplace disaster preparedness activities. Most employers are required to provide emergency plans and procedures by OSHA. Find out what programs your employer has and get involved.

• If your employer does not have any programs, talk to your human resources department about what can be done to start a program.

• For students or those with children in school, find out what they have to offer for disaster plans, training, or exercises.

• Health club members are encouraged to inquire if they offer CPR or first aid training. By law, health clubs are required to have an Automated External Defibrillator (AED) and trained staff on the premise in case of an emergency.

• Contact your local Red Cross, to ask which companies and schools are included in their Ready When the Time Comes and Ready Rating programs. These programs provide volunteer opportunities for businesses and schools that include CPR/First Aid and other types of disaster training.

• If the local church has a health and wellness ministry, inquire about training opportunities that may be available. If they do not have a ministry that focuses on family wellness, start one. There are many free sources to help in this regard. Use the internet to look up local organizations that offer training in disaster preparedness or response.

• Find out whether your church has a disaster plan or evacuation plan. If not, develop one. The Resource Guide in this book will provide more information about organizations that can help provide information for program development.

In an emergency, only three things are going to matter:

✓ Where will I go?

✓ What should I do?

✓ How can I help my family and neighbors survive?

Knowing the answer to these questions is the essence of disaster preparedness. Disaster preparedness is nothing more than having a plan, and a method for executing the plan under the worst possible circumstances. One cannot possibly prepare for every disaster that could occur; therefore, an all-hazards approach should be used when making plans and preparations.

Regardless of the disaster, if one is ready to help themselves, their chances of survival are vastly improved.

CHAPTER 10

CONCLUSION

"For God has not given us a spirit of fear,
but of power and of love and of a sound mind."

2 Timothy 1:6-8.

What can the underserved do to help themselves cope with disasters? Some insist they must be financially stable before they can handle the devastating effects of catastrophes. The reality is until we empower the least able among us with skills, training, and a different sense of destiny; we will never close the disaster gap between underserved communities and mainstream America. Fundamental change can occur in underserved communities when attitudes change. All stakeholders, government, private sector, nongovernment organizations, and yes, the underserved must step up to the challenges of preparedness.

The late pop icon Michael Jackson's song *"Man in the Mirror"* said it best. It starts with us, individually and collectively. We must embrace new ideas and ways of doing things when it comes to preparedness. Taking charge and attacking apathy and indifference is the only realistic option for the underserved.

In order to accomplish these goals, underserved communities must:

1. Break the cycle of emotional dependency on government, in which they view themselves as "victims" rather than survivors.

2. Be realistic about their role and responsibility to overcome misconceptions and misinformation about disaster preparedness.

3. Get in the game with respect to disaster planning and use all the available resources to increase knowledge and awareness about disasters

4. Put faith principles to work when preparing for disasters and do not be content in the "victim" role.

The underlying foundation for achieving preparedness for those who need it the most must be firmly grounded in faith. Simply put, we must believe in a different outcome before we can achieve it.

Leaders in every community must make it a priority to prepare underserved constituents by practicing inclusiveness. They must start by incorporating vulnerable populations into realistic drills and exercises, and promoting preparedness as a way of life in churches, families, and neighborhoods. If we can achieve small successes such as developing a community wide preparedness plan, victory is assured.

There is an old saying that goes, I never see failure as failure, but merely the negative feedback I need to change course in my direction. If we have not learned from the debacle of Hurricane Katrina, and other catastrophes, we are only one step away from repeating the mistakes that caused loss of life, and needless suffering.

Ultimately, however, it is up to those in the local community who are engaged as disaster preparedness planners and responders, to elevate the discourse. They must become advocates for the underserved at the local, state, and national levels. If these voices of change can come together to turn passion into action, real change will occur. We can and will be better prepared in the future to achieve a more equitable response to disasters.

As this author observed the helicopters rescuing people from rooftops in New Orleans, it brought to mind my own grandmother, Lucille Franklin. She lived out her final years in a nursing home, where she passed away peacefully in her sleep at age 99. Suffering from dementia and other ills that inevitably come to pass in a life that spanned nearly a century, my grandmother dedicated her entire life to her family, raising five daughters during the Great Depression. Her life was marked by suffering and sacrifice. The legacy she left for my family is a rich tradition of faith and service to others. The thought of a Katrina grandmother, gripped by sheer panic, strapped to a bed as a deluge of muddy water overtook her final breath, is completely unacceptable. Why prepare for disasters? Because we owe it to our families, and neighbors to ensure their lives are valued and honored. Preventable tragedies like those which have occurred in the past should never be allowed to happen again. Victory is ours if we are willing to prepare for the unexpected tragedies of life. Only after we have done all we can to help ourselves, can we truly leave the outcome to the Creator.

RESOURCE GUIDE

Note: this list represents a sample for suggested groups to consider for planning. Additional groups may be desired to achieve planning goals.

Citizen Corps

Citizen Corps encourages citizens to engage in a number of activities to help prepare themselves and their communities:

Personal Preparedness: Developing a household preparedness plan and disaster supplies kits, observing home health and safety practices, implementing disaster mitigation measures, and participating in crime prevention and reporting.

Training: Taking classes in emergency preparedness, response capabilities, first aid, CPR, fire suppression, and search and rescue procedures.

Volunteer Service: Engaging individuals in volunteer activities that support first responders, disaster relief groups, and community safety organizations.

The program is coordinated nationally by the Department of Homeland Security. In this capacity, the Department of Homeland Security works closely with other federal entities, state and local governments, first responders and emergency managers, the volunteer community, and the White House Office of the USA

Freedom Corps.

Citizen Corps Partner Programs

The Department of Homeland Security, the Department of Justice, and the Department of Health and Human Services jointly administer five programs through Citizen Corps.

Community Emergency Response Team

Specially administered by the Department of Homeland Security, the Community Emergency Response Team (CERT) program educates the American public about disaster preparedness and sponsors training of basic emergency skills such as fire suppression, search and rescue (SAR) and handling mass casualty. The CERT program emphasizes working in conjunction with professional responders and community organizations to assist in emergency and event management. CERT programs are typically sponsored by local or county offices of Emergency Management. CERT programs seek to create a mindset shift within the psyche of the American public from a response culture to a preparedness culture through community outreach and education.

Fire Corps

Fire Corps seeks to bolster local fire departments with

volunteer firefighters in order to more effectively contain disasters. These "citizen advocates" also assist in community fire safety outreach, youth programs, and administrative support. The Fire Corps is funded through the Department of Homeland Security and is managed and implemented by the National Volunteer Fire Council, in partnership with the International Association of Fire Fighters, the International Association of Fire Chiefs, and other groups that make up the National Advisory Committee.

Neighborhood Watch

An expanded Neighborhood Watch Program (NWP) Program incorporates terrorism awareness education into its existing crime prevention mission, while also serving as a way to bring residents together to focus on emergency preparedness and emergency response training. Funded by DOJ, Neighborhood Watch is administered by the National Sheriffs' Association.

Medical Reserve Corps

The Medical Reserve Corps (MRC) Program strengthens communities by helping medical, public health and other volunteers offer their expertise throughout the year as well as during local emergencies and other times of community need. MRC volunteers work in coordination with existing local emergency response programs and also supplement existing community public health initiatives, such as outreach and prevention, immunization programs, blood drives, case management, care planning, and other efforts. The MRC program is administered by HHS.

Volunteers in Police Program

Volunteers in Police Service (VIPS) work to enhance the capacity of state and local law enforcement to utilize volunteers. VIPS serves as a gateway to resources and information for and about law enforcement volunteer programs. Funded by DOJ, VIPS is managed and implemented by International Association of Chiefs of Police. Affiliated organizations

The Citizen Corps Affiliate Program expands the resources and materials available to states and local communities by partnering with Programs and Organizations that offer resources for public education, outreach, and training; represent volunteers interested in helping to make their community safer; or offer volunteer service opportunities to support first responders, disaster relief activities, and community safety efforts.

The following previously existing non-governmental preparedness programs are partners in the Citizen Corps Program:

The American Association of Community Colleges

The American Association of Community Colleges is the

primary advocacy organization for the nation's community colleges, representing almost 1,200 two-year institutions and more than 11 million students. Nationally, community colleges enroll almost half (46%) of all U.S. undergraduates. Community colleges have taken the lead in Homeland Security Education, with over 80% of police, fire and EMTs receiving their credentials from these institutions. AACC supports their membership through policy initiatives, innovative programs, research and information, professional development and other efforts.

The American Legion

Given a congressional charter in 1919, The American Legion serves as an advocate for American's veterans, a friend of the U.S. military, a sponsor of community-based programs for young people, and a spokesman for patriotic values. Nearly 2.7 million men and women who served in the U.S. military during an official period of conflict are members, making The American Legion the nation's largest veterans groups, with approximately 14,500 American Legion Posts worldwide.

The American Legion Auxiliary

The American Legion Auxiliary is the largest patriotic women's service organization in the world, with nearly 1 million members. Affiliated with The American Legion and chartered by

Congress in 1920, the Auxiliary is a veterans' service organization with members in nearly 10,000 American communities. The organization sponsors volunteer programs on the national and local levels, focusing on three major areas: veterans, young people and the community.

American Red Cross

For more than 122 years, the mission of the American Red Cross has been to help people prevent, prepare for, and respond to emergencies. A humanitarian organization led by volunteers, guided by its Congressional Charter and the Fundamental Principles of the International Red Cross Movement, the ARC is woven into the fabric of our communities with 940 chapters nationwide. In fulfilling its mission, ARC is empowering Americans to take practical steps to make families, neighborhoods, schools and workplaces safer, healthier and more resilient in the face of adversity. Through the Together We Prepare program, the ARC provides training for the public in community disaster preparedness and response; and lifesaving skills training (First Aid and CPR). The program also encourages people to donate blood and volunteer to help build community preparedness.

American Radio Relay League

The American Radio Relay League is a non-commercial

membership association of amateur radio operators organized for the promotion of interest in Amateur Radio communication and experimentation, for the establishment of networks to provide communications in the event of disasters or other emergencies, for the advancement of the public welfare, for the representation of the Radio Amateur in legislative and regulatory matters. ARRL is the principal organization representing the interests of the more than 650,000 U.S. Radio Amateurs. Because of its organized emergency communications capability, ARRL's Amateur Radio Emergency Service (ARES) can be of valuable assistance in providing critical and essential communications during emergencies and disasters when normal lines of communication are disrupted. ARRL conducts emergency communications training and certifies proficiency in emergency communications skills.

Association of Public Television Stations (APTS)

The Association of Public Television Stations is a nonprofit membership organization established in 1980 to support the continued growth and development of a strong and financially sound noncommercial television service for the American public. APTS provides advocacy for public television interests at the national level, as well as consistent leadership and information in marshaling support for its members: the nation's 356 public television stations.

Civil Air Patrol

Civil Air Patrol is a congressionally chartered, non-profit corporation and is the civilian auxiliary of the U.S. Air Force available to any department or agency in any branch of the Federal Government. Its corporate purposes include being an organization to encourage and develop by example the voluntary contribution of private citizens to the public welfare and to provide private citizens with adequate facilities to assist in meeting local and national emergencies. It does this, in part, by providing aerospace education, cadet training, and emergency response services through 1,600 local units nationwide. CAP supports Homeland Security efforts through memoranda of understanding with various federal, state and local government agencies under which its volunteer members provide air/ground search and rescue, coastal patrol, air/ground observation, radio communications and relay, aerial reconnaissance, air-to-ground photography, radiological monitoring, and disaster and damage assessment assets.

E9-1-1 Institute

E9-1-1 Institute is a non-profit organization that supports the Congressional E9-1-1 Caucus in promoting public education on E9-1-1 and emergency communications issues. The Congressional E9-1-1 Caucus was formed as a joint initiative to educate lawmakers, constituents, and committees about the importance of citizen-activated emergency response systems. E9-1-1 Institute serves as an information clearinghouse for policy makers at the federal, state, and local levels, as well as for interested parties and the general public. E-911 Institute is supported through member donations. Environmental Protection Agency

The United States Environmental Protection Agency's (EPA) mission is to protect public health and to safeguard the natural environment. EPA provides leadership in the area of chemical safety through State Emergency Response Commissions (SERCs) and Local Emergency Planning Committees (LEPCs), which receive, manage, and use information about chemical hazards in the community to make residents safer.

Home Safety Council

The Home Safety Council is a non-profit organization dedicated to helping prevent the nearly 21 million medical visits that occur on average each year from unintentional injuries in the home. Through national programs and partners across America, the HSC works to educate and empower families to take actions that help keep them safer in and around their homes. Through its charitable and educational projects, the HSC works with national safety-related organizations, home products suppliers, school systems, local fire departments, and volunteers across the country to improve home safety.

Meals on Wheels Association of America

Meals on Wheels Association of America is the oldest and largest organization in the United States representing those who provide meal services to people in need. MOWAA works toward the social, physical, nutritional, and economic betterment of vulnerable Americans. With the guiding principle to help those men and women who are elderly, homebound, disabled, frail, or at risk, MOWAA provides the tools and information its state and local programs need to make a difference in the lives of others. It also gives cash grants to local senior meal programs throughout the country to assist in providing meals and other nutrition services.

Mercy Medical Airlift

Mercy Medical Airlift is a non-profit organization dedicated to providing charitable, long-distance air transportation ensuring patient access to distant specialized medical evaluation, diagnosis, and treatment. MMA is totally supported through charitable giving and the services of volunteer pilots and office assistants. Volunteer pilots link with other pilots nationally - together flying multiple thousands of needy patients each year. In times of emergency, volunteer pilots working within the Homeland Security Emergency Air Transportation System (HSEATS) program stand ready to transport small priority cargo and key emergency management personnel to needed destinations.

MyGoodDeed.org

The mission of MyGoodDeed.org is to transform 9/11 into an annually recognized national day of voluntary service, and give individuals and organizations the power through dynamic online networking to make a difference in the world, one good deed at a time. Created by 9/11 families and friends shortly after the terrorist attacks on America, MyGoodDeed.org seeks to honor the thousands who were killed and injured on 9/11, to pay tribute to the many who aided in the rescue and recovery efforts, and to remember and rekindle the remarkable spirit of unity that existed in our nation in the days following 9/11. MyGoodDeed.org has developed a social cause online networking website to connect people with common social interests and to encourage participation in community service around 9/11 and throughout the year.

National Association for Search and Rescue

The National Association for Search and Rescue is a non-profit membership association dedicated to advancing professional, literary, and scientific knowledge in search and rescue and related fields. NASAR is composed of thousands of paid and non-paid professionals interested in all aspects of search and rescue throughout the United States and around the world. NASAR has trained over 30,000 responders since 1989 utilizing its internationally respected SARTECH© Certification Program. NASAR is dedicated to ensuring that volunteers (non-paid professionals) in search and rescue are as prepared as the career public safety personnel (fire, law and emergency medical services) with whom they work on a daily basis. National Crime Prevention Council

The National Crime Prevention Council mission is to enable people to create safer and more caring communities by addressing the causes of crime and violence and reducing the opportunities for crime to occur. NCPC publishes books, kits of camera-ready program materials, posters, and informational and policy reports on a variety of crime prevention and community-building subjects and hosts websites that offer crime prevention tips for individuals and communities. NCPC offers training, technical assistance, and a national focus for crime prevention: it acts as secretariat for the Crime Prevention Coalition of America. It operates demonstration programs in schools, neighborhoods, and entire jurisdictions and takes a major leadership role in youth crime prevention and youth service; it also administers the Center for Faith and Service. NCPC manages the McGruff Take A Bite Out Of Crime public service advertising campaign.

National Fire Protection Association

The National Fire Protection Association is an international non-profit organization that seeks to reduce the burden of fire and other hazards on the quality of life by providing and advocating scientifically-based consensus codes and standards, research, training, and education.

National Oceanic and Atmospheric Administration

NOAA conducts research and gathers data about the global oceans, atmosphere, space, and sun, and applies this knowledge to science and service that touch the lives of all Americans. NOAA's National Weather Service is the primary source of weather data, forecasts and warnings for the United States. The NWS is the sole United States official voice for issuing warnings during life threatening weather situations and operates the NOAA Weather Radio network, which broadcasts weather and other hazard warnings, watches, forecasts and post-event information 24 hours a day.

National Safety Council

The National Safety Council is a congressionally chartered national organization with a mission to educate and influence society to adopt safety, health, and environmental policies, practices, and procedures that prevent and mitigate human suffering and economic losses arising from preventable causes. The mission encompasses unintentional injuries on the job; highway, community and recreation safety; and all major causes of preventable injuries and deaths, including occupational and environmental health and general wellness. Along with its national advocacy, the Council carries out its mission on the community level through a network of Chapters, which are dedicated to promoting safety and health in all walks of life, 24 hours a day.

National Volunteer Fire Council

The National Volunteer Fire Council (NVFC) is a non-profit membership association representing the interests of the volunteer fire, EMS, and rescue service. The NVFC promotes and provides education and training for volunteer fire and EMS organizations, and provides representation on national standards setting committees and projects. NVFC also operates 1-800-FIRE-LINE, a toll free number which links interested citizens with volunteer emergency opportunities in their community.

National Voluntary Organizations Active in Disaster

The National Voluntary Organizations Active in Disaster (NVOAD) is coalition of the major national voluntary organizations that have made disaster related work a priority. With 33 years of respected experience, the NVOAD member agencies provide skilled direct services along the continuum from disaster prevention and preparation to response, recovery and mitigation. NVOAD serves its member agencies by coordinating planning efforts, enhancing response capabilities, and, when an incident occurs, facilitating comprehensive, coordinated volunteer response in partnership with emergency managers. This cooperative effort has proven to be the most effective way for a wide variety of volunteers and organizations to work together in a crisis. Throughout the year, NVOAD members work to foster cooperation, coordination, communication and collaboration among the member agencies and with government and private sector partners.

Operation HOPE, Inc.

Operation HOPE, Inc. (OHI) is a non-profit organization providing economic education for America's inner city communities. HOPE Coalition America (HCA) is an initiative of OHI, which provides free and compassionate economic counseling to businesses and families to help them prepare for and recover from major disasters or emergencies. Created after the September 11th attack on America and supported by America's leading financial institutions, HCA serves as a resource network of banking, financial services, legal, insurance, higher education, social service, and community development professionals committed to providing practical information and tools for disaster planning and to helping those affected by disaster rebuild their financial life. One such tool is the Emergency Financial First Aid Kit (EFFAK) (PDF), which helps uses identify and organize key financial records to minimize the financial impact of a natural disaster or national emergency.

Points of Light Foundation and the HandsOn Network

Points of Light Institute was created by the merger of the Points of Light Foundation and HandsOn Network in August 2007. The result is a powerful, integrated national organization with a global focus to redefine volunteerism and civic engagement for the 21st century, putting people at the center of community problem solving. To realize this vision, Points of Light Institute operates three dynamic business units that share a mission to inspire, equip and mobilize people to take action that changes the world; HandsOn Network, Mission Fish and Civic Incubator, which provide a variety of ways for people to participate in local, national and global communities. HandsOn Network, the leading business unit and activating, volunteer-focused arm of Points of Light Institute, creates opportunities for people and organizations to apply their interests and passions to make a difference in their communities. At the center of HandsOn Network are nearly 250 affiliates that service in all 50 states and 12 international communities in nine countries.

United States Department of Education, Office of Safe and Drug Free Schools

OSDFS administers, coordinates, and recommends policy for improving the quality and excellence of programs and activities that are designed to provide financial and technical assistance for drug and violence prevention and to promote the health and well-being of students in elementary and secondary schools and institutions of higher education. Additional areas of focus include student-led crime prevention; health, mental health, environmental health, and physical education programs; crisis planning and emergency planning, including natural disasters, violent incidents and terrorist acts; and programs relating to citizenship and civics education.

United States Junior Chamber

The mission of Jaycees is to provide young people the opportunity to develop personal and leadership skills through local community action and organizational involvement while expanding the Junior Chamber movement. Through local chapters, the Jaycees have a long history of building and supporting communities across the nation, from playgrounds and parks to disaster relief. In today's environment, all Jaycees and their chapters are being called to action to help step-up America's homeland security efforts. Through their affiliation with Citizen Corps, the Jaycees will promote the formation of local Citizen Corps Councils through local Jaycee chapter participation and will assist these Councils with implementing the programs and practices associated with Citizen Corps.

Veterans of Foreign Wars

The VFW is the nation's oldest major organization serving veterans and their communities. The 2.6 million members of the VFW and its auxiliaries have a rich tradition of enhancing the lives of millions through its community service programs and special projects. A commitment to volunteerism is a cornerstone of the VFW, with a particular focus on programs that build stronger communities by promoting education, civic pride, civic responsibility and an appreciation for America's history and traditions.

Disaster Relief (National Organizations)

- Adventist Community Services

- American Baptist Men

- American Radio Relay League

- American Red Cross

- Brethren Disaster Ministries

- Catholic Charities, USA

- Christian Disaster Response International

- Christian Reformed World Relief Committee

- Church World Service

- Churches of Scientology Disaster Response

- City Team Ministries

- Convoy of Hope

- Episcopal Relief and Development

- Feeding America (Formerly America's Second Harvest)

- Feed the Children

- Habitat for Humanity International

- Hope Coalition America

- The Humane Society of the United States

- International Aid

- International Critical Incident Stress Foundation

- International Organization for Victim Assistance

- International Relief and Development

- International Relief Friendship Foundation

- Latter Day Charities

- Lutheran Disaster Response

- Mennonite Disaster Service

- Mercy Medical Airlift/Angel Flight America

- National Association of Jewish Chaplains

- National Emergency Response Teams (NERT)

- National Organization for Victim Assistance

- Nazarene Disaster Response

- Noah's Wish - Animal Disaster Response

- Operation Blessing International

- Presbyterian Disaster Assistance

- REACT International

- The Salvation Army

- Samaritan's Purse

- Save the Children

- Society of St. Vincent de Paul

- Southern Baptist Convention –North American Mission Board

- Taiwan Buddhist Tzu Chi Foundation USA

- United Church of Christ –Wider Church Ministries

- United Jewish Communities

- United Methodist Committee on Relief (UMCOR)

- United Way of America

- Volunteers of America

- World Vision

Educational

- Colleges and universities

- Public & Private Schools K-12

- Child care facilities (both center-based and home-based)

Governmental

- Health departments (local, county, state)

- Departments of Education

- Health and human services agencies (including child welfare)

- HUD or other rent-subsidized multi-family complexes

- HUD or other subsidized non-licensed supervised living facilities

- Governor's committees on individuals with special needs and/or disabilities (as applicable)

Human Services

- Agencies on alcohol and drug addiction

- Job and family service agencies.

- Departments of aging and social services

- Vocational rehabilitation agencies

Nongovernmental

- Culturally based community groups

- Faith-based organizations

- Community activist groups

Medical

- Hospitals and hospices

- Home healthcare organizations

- Medical service and equipment providers (including durable medical equipment providers)

- Pharmaceutical providers

Mental Health

- Behavioral health and mental health agencies

- Private mental health organizations

Functional and Accessible Needs

- Commissions on the deaf and hard of hearing and the blind and visually impaired

- Local government and nongovernment disability agencies

- Nursing homes

- Independent living centers

- Translation and interpretation service agencies

- Developmental disabilities networks and service providers

- Individuals with functional needs

Other

- Transportation service providers (including those with

accessible vehicles)

- Social Media

- Parents organizations

- Private sector companies

- Philanthropic organizations

WORKS CITED

"Alpha Public Health Forum." (n.d.): n. page. 2007. Web.

"CBS News." CBS News. CBS Interactive, 11 Feb. 2009. Web. 12 July 2012. <http://www.cbsnews.com/2100-224_162-553391.html>.

Centers for Disease Control and Prevention. Centers for Disease Control and Prevention, n.d. Web. Jan.-Feb. 2012. <http://www.cdc.gov/>.

"CMAP." GO TO 2040. N.P., n.d. Web. 12 July 2012. <http://www.cmap.illinois.gov/2040/main>.

"Disasters - Are We Prepared." Up Front with Jesse Jackson. Word Network. Chicago, IL, 30 Jan. 2009. Television.

Davis Vincent B. /SALF "Save A Life Foundation Responds to Latest Attack by ABC-7 Reporter." -- Re CHICAGO, June 8 /PRNewswire-US Newswire/ --. N.P., 8 June 2007.

"Emergency Preparedness and Response." CDC Emergency Preparedness & Response Site. N.P., n.d. Web. Spring 2012. <http://www.bt.cdc.gov/>.

Faith-Ba Evans-Holland, Myrtle. "Perceived Preparedness and Preparedness Behavior for Terrorism and Natural Disasters among Low-income African-Americans in Maryland." Diss. N.d. Abstract. (2009): n. page. Print sed Partners.

Holy Bible 2 Timothy. N.P.: N.P., n.d. Print

Holy Bible "Genesis 8:1." N.P.: N.P., n.d. N. page. Print

Illinois Department of Public Health: Faith-Based Emergency Preparedness Initiative. <http://www.idph.state.il.us/planready/fbp.htm>.

"FEMA | Federal Emergency Management Agency." FEMA | Federal Emergency Management Agency. N.P., n.d. Web. Aug.-Sept. 2011. <http://www.fema.gov/>.

Health Alert Network. Centers for Disease Control, n.d. Web. Spring 2012. <http://www2a.cdc.gov/han/index.asp>.

"Illinois Faith-Based Emergency Preparedness Initiative." Illinois Faith-Based Emergency Preparedness Initiative. Illinois Department of Public Health May-June 2007. Web. Nov.-Dec. 2011. <http://www.idph.state.il.us/planready/prepare.htm.

Koenig, Harold G. In the Wake of Disaster: Religious Responses to Terrorism & Catastrophe. Philadelphia: Templeton Foundation, 2006. Print.

McEnaney, Laura. Civil Defense Begins at Home: Militarization Meets Everyday Life in the Fifties. Princeton, NJ [u.a.: Princeton Univ., 2000. Print.

"Preparedness and Emergency Response Learning Center." - Harvard School of Public Health. N.P., n.d. Web. Spring 2012. <http://www.hsph.harvard.edu/hperlc>.

Press release. Comprehensive Preparedness Guide 301: Special Needs Planning. 15 Aug. 2008. Federal Emergency Management Agency. <http://www.fema.gov/news/newsrelease.fema?id=45436>.

Public Readiness Index Chicago. Rep. Council for Excellence in Government: Conducted by Schulman, Ronca and Bucuvalas, Inc., December 13, 2006.

Public Readiness Index Chicago: Telephone survey of 1,006 U.S. Adults 18 years and older. Rep. Chicago Council for Excellence in Government: Conducted by ORC International, July 10-13, 2008.

Interview. Identifying Who Survives Disasters And Why. National Public Radio. Book Tour, Washington, D.C. 22 July 2008. <http://www.npr.org/templates/story/story.php?storyId=92616679 >

Parker, Laura. "Louisiana Nursing Home Case Puts Katrina Response on Trial." USA Today. Gannett, 9 Aug. 2007. Web. 12 July 2012. <http://www.usatoday.com/news/nation/2007-08-08-1Acover_N.htm>.

Ripley, Amanda. The Unthinkable: Who Survives When Disaster Strikes and Why? New York: Crown, 2008. Print.

Save-A-Life Foundation. Www.salf.org. N.P., 2005. Web.

Steinberg, Theodore. Acts of God: The Unnatural History of Natural Disaster in America. New York: Oxford UP, 2000. Print.

"Suburbs Not Likely to Get U.S. Flood Aid." Chicago Tribune. N.P., 24 June 2004. Web. 12 July 2012. <http://articles.chicagotribune.com/2004-06-4/news/0406240259_1_federal-aid-flood-disaster-areas>.

"2010 Census." 2010 Census. N.P., 2010. Web. 12 July 2012. <http://2010.census.gov/2010census/>.

Taylor-Thompson, Cheryl. African-Americans & Terrorism." Alpha Public Health Forum, Baltimore. 2007.

Lecture "The Legacy of Katrina's Children: Estimating the numbers of at-risk children in the Gulf Coast states of Louisiana and Mississippi," D Abramson, I Redlener, T Stehling-Ariza, E Fuller, National Center for Disaster Preparedness, Research Brief 2007:12. Columbia University Mailman School of Public Health, New York. (7 Dec 2007) Prepared by the National Center for Disaster Preparedness at Columbia University.

Amazon.com: Acts of God: The Unnatural History of Natural .., http://www.amazon.com/Acts-God-Unnatural-History-Disaster/dp/0195142632 (accessed September 10, 2012).

"United States Citizenship and Immigration Services (USCIS ..." Insert Name of Site in Italics. N.p., n.d. Web. 10 Sept. 2012 <http://www.thecertifiedtranslation.com/USCIS-requirements-certified-translation.

The Poorest Counties in America – Main Street, http://www.mainstreet.com/slideshow/moneyinvesting/news/poorest-counties-america (accessed September 10, 2012).

Perceived preparedness and preparedness behavior for .., http://udini.proquest.com/view/perceived-preparedness-and-pqid:1980468921/ (accessed September 10, 2012).

Natural Hazards Observer - March 2001 - University of ... (n.d.). Retrieved from http://www.colorado.edu/hazards/o/archives/2001/mar01/mar01d.html

Perceived preparedness and preparedness behavior for ... (n.d.). Retrieved from http://udini.proquest.com/view/perceived-preparedness-and-pqid:1980468921/

United States Citizenship and Immigration Services (USCIS ... (n.d.). Retrieved from http://www.thecertifiedtranslation.com/USCIS-requirements-certified-translation.php

The Poorest Counties in America – Main Street. (n.d.). Retrieved from http://www.mainstreet.com/slideshow/moneyinvesting/news/poorest-counties-america

HUD's FOIA Regulations - HUD. (n.d.). Retrieved from http://portal.hud.gov/hudportal/HUD?src=/program_offices/administration/foia/foi

http://portal.hud.gov/hudportal/HUD?src=/program_offices/administration/foia/foi...

Katrina Nursing Home Owners Acquitted - CBS News. (n.d.). Retrieved from http://www.cbsnews.com/2100-201_162-3243854.html

Hurricane Katrina - Wikipedia, the free encyclopedia. (n.d.). Retrieved from http://en.wikipedia.org/wiki/Hurricane_Katrina

The American Preparedness Project. (n.d.). Retrieved from http://ncdp.mailman.columbia.edu/files/Marist2011.pdf

Trader-Leigh, Karyn. 2007. Understanding the role of African American Churches and Clergy in Community Crisis response. Washington, DC: Joint Center for Political and Economic Studies, p. 3. 1

Morse, Reilly. 2007. Environmental Justice through the Eye of Hurricane Katrina. Washington, DC

ABOUT THE AUTHOR

A native of Maywood Illinois, Vincent Davis began his emergency management career in the Illinois National Guard, where he served a distinguished 23-year career before retiring in 2001. Mr. Davis served as External Affairs and Community Relations manager at FEMA Region V, where he led field teams' deployed for11 Presidential disasters. In 2004, he supervised community relations teams in Florida and Alabama and served on a task force at FEMA HQ coordinating training and deployment for 5,000 Citizen Corps volunteers assigned to the Gulf region during Hurricanes Charlie, Frances, Ivan, and Jeanne.

After leaving FEMA, he served as National Director of Operations for the Save-A-Life Foundation, managing programs providing CPR and first aid training for school children. Later, as Regional Preparedness Manager for the American Red Cross of Greater Chicago, Mr. Davis oversaw research and development of the groundbreaking Regional Emergency Preparedness Report for the Chicago Metropolitan Agency for Planning (CMAP) Go To 2040 Project. As a consultant, Mr. Davis played a pivotal role in developing the Regional Catastrophic Incident Coordination Plan for FEMA in 2011. This effort involved coordinating and establishing catastrophic disaster plans for evacuation, mass care, public information, and logistics for 16 counties and the City of Chicago. Regarded as a subject-matter-expert in preparedness planning, Mr. Davis holds numerous certifications in emergency management planning, training, exercises, public affairs, community relations, and incident management. Mr. Davis currently serves as Program Manager in the Emergency Preparedness and Response division for Walgreens Family of Companies.